APPRAISING EDUCATIONAL RESEARCH:

A Case Study Approach

JASON MILLMAN and D. BOB GOWIN

Cornell University

PRENTICE-HALL, INC., *Englewood Cliffs, N.J.*

Library of Congress Cataloging in Publication Data

MILLMAN, JASON, COMP.
  Appraising educational research.

  (Prentice-Hall series in educational measurement, research, and statistics)
  Includes bibliographical references.
  1. Educational research—Case studies.
2. Education—Addresses, essays, lectures.
I. Gowin, D.B., joint comp. II. Title.
LB1028.M49   370'.78   73–18004
ISBN 0-13-043638-0

PRENTICE-HALL SERIES IN
EDUCATIONAL MEASUREMENT, RESEARCH, AND STATISTICS

Gene V Glass, *Editor*

1974.

Printed in the United States of America

10   9   8   7   6   5

PRENTICE-HALL INTERNATIONAL, INC., *London*
PRENTICE-HALL OF AUSTRALIA, PTY, LTD., *Sydney*
PRENTICE-HALL OF CANADA, LTD., *Toronto*
PRENTICE-HALL OF INDIA PRIVATE LIMITED, *New Delhi*
PRENTICE-HALL OF JAPAN, INC., *Tokyo*

Contents

Preface   v

1
The Nature of Criticism   1

2
Eight Research Articles and Critiques:
Description and Suggestions for Using Them   6

3
Do Grades Stimulate Students to Failure?   9
 Charles H. Josephson
CRITIQUE, 14

4
"Head Start" Experience and the Development
of Skills and Abilities in Kindergarten Children   23
 Eleanor S. Kaplan
CRITIQUE, 40

5

Prediction of Long-Term Success in
Doctoral Work in Psychology   *51*
J. Richard Hackman / Nancy Wiggins
Alan R. Bass
CRITIQUE,   57

6

The Influence of Analysis and Evaluation Questions
On Achievement in Sixth Grade Social Studies   *74*
Francis P. Hunkins
CRITIQUE,   81

7

Effects of Positive Social Reinforcement
on Regressed Crawling of a Nursery School Child   *98*
Florence R. Harris / Margaret K. Johnston
C. Susan Kelley / Montrose M. Wolf
CRITIQUE,   106

8

Motivation and Creativity: The Context Effect   *115*
David Elkind / Joann Deblinger
David Adler
CRITIQUE,   120

9

Tampering with Nature
in Elementary School Science   *151*
Joanne Reynolds Bronars
CRITIQUE,   155

10

Effects of Hierarchical Differentiation on Group
Productivity, Efficiency, and Risk Taking   *164*
Edwin M. Bridges / Wayne J. Doyle
David J. Mahan
CRITIQUE,   174

Preface

A surprising fact to us is that the tradition of critical appraisal is so largely missing in the context of educational research. Very little good criticism of educational research occurs. Why?

Perhaps it is a matter of assumed senatorial courtesy or that the best criticism of other research is simply doing a superior piece of research, or that since educators are dedicated, good people one should not be critical, or that a sharp-eyed critic is a dangerous fellow because he will embarrass a naive or foolish empiricist, or possibly that research is done to achieve tenure, promotion, increase in salary, prestige, esteem, more grants, and so forth. These reasons and others much gossiped about at research meetings do not really concern us. We think both research and criticism are matters that intelligent students can be expertly trained to do well, and we see no reason not to try to improve present practices. One need not be afraid of criticism.

Very little good material is available as instruction in criticism. We do think that good criticism is needed in education and this fact has led us to put forth the effort recorded here.

This book has a rare characteristic: the eight critiques which comprise the main contribution have been extensively field-tested. The critiques were developed and modified on the basis of comments supplied by over 800 students from 27 colleges and universities. Indispensable to us were the reactions of subject-matter experts and of students participating in the successive field tryouts. The cycle of field test–modify–field test–modify permitted the materials to achieve a level of quality not possible otherwise.

Acknowledgment of the help of several groups is in order. Specifically, we owe much to:

1. the students and cooperating professors of the following institutions: Arizona State University, C. W. Post, Catholic University of America, Cornell University, Creighton University, Eastern Kentucky University, George Washington University, Kansas State University, Montclair State College, Ohio State University, Pennsylvania State University, Purdue University, St. Louis University, Stanford University, Towson State, University of Colorado, University of Georgia, University of Louisville, University of Maryland, University of Nevada at Reno, University of New Mexico, University of Northern Iowa, University of Southwestern Louisiana, University of Washington, University of Wisconsin at Madison, University of Wisconsin at Milwaukee, and The College of William and Mary.

2. the following scholars who supplied us with an initial reaction to one of the articles: David Farr and John Milholland (Chapter 3), Gene Glass (Chapter 4), Leonard Krimerman (Chapter 5), Kenneth Hopkins and William Lowe (Chapter 6), Alberta Siegal and Harold Stevenson (Chapter 7), J. P. Guilford and Kenneth Strike (Chapter 8), John Easley and Jonas Soltis (Chapter 9), and W. W. Charters, Jr. and Robert Ennis (Chapter 10).[1]

3. the following professionally-minded investigators who offered constructive reactions to our critiques of or further information about their research articles: Edwin M. Bridges, Joanne Reynolds Bronars, Wayne Doyle, David Elkind, J. Richard Hackman, Charles H. Josephson, and David Mahan.[1]

4. the publishers and investigators who were willing to grant permission to reproduce their articles despite the presence of negative comments.

5. the United States Office of Education and Cornell University which provided financial support for development of these materials.

6. Prentice-Hall for making it possible for these training materials to be disseminated.

JASON MILLMAN

D. BOB GOWIN

---

[1] Acknowledgment of the assistance of the scholars and investigators named above should not be construed to mean that they approve of all aspects of our appraisals.

1

The Nature
of
Criticism

There is a sense in which the critical appraisal of empirical research papers is also an act of research. It is an act of research because the critic contemplates each of the aspects of the research papers very much as the original author did. The key elements in the pattern of inquiry are the same for both the doing of research and the doing of criticism. In either, one must take a look at the nature of the problem, the phenomena of interest, the telling question, the key concepts, the methods of work, the knowledge claims and other products of the research effort, and the value or significance of the research.

The act of critical appraisal is a process of analysis, of breaking down and taking apart what was produced by an act of synthesis by the original author. The critic brings another pair of eyes, another mind, another point of view to the research. Specific training in criticism will in the long run enhance actual research.

Each element in the pattern of inquiry requires the investigator to select, arrange, modify, and interpret. This process requires judgments. For example, the selection of phenomena of interest and from that the setting up of a problem involve a judgment that these aspects of the world of experience are worth inquiring into, implicitly rejecting other concerns that might be worked on. The precise form of the telling question is a judgment that this question and not some other question will enable the researcher to find something of importance. The use of one set of key concepts to ask the telling question means that other concepts have been thought about and rejected for the time being. The research design, the selection of specific techniques of data gathering, statistical analysis, the construction of tables and graphs and other ways of presenting the record of the research effort are based on the judgment that these methods are better than others that might be used. Finally, the particular knowledge claims selected as the important ones, the conclusions that are interpreted by the researchers, signify yet another set of judgments about what is worth reporting and what is seen as having value to other researchers.

The categories of critical appraisal are basically no different from the categories of actual inquiry. The critic should question the judgments made at each stage of inquiry. Specifically, he should ask: What other phenomena of interest might be relevant? What other way to pose the problem could be thought of? What different concepts or conceptual systems might have been used? What alternative designs or methods or techniques for data gathering could have been considered? What limits to generalization are found in the particular way the research is reported? What other values might conceivably be found in this research? Critical appraisal, like worthwhile research, depends heavily on human judgment.

THREE PURPOSES OF CRITICISM

First, to the extent that educational research is an attempt to establish the fundamental and foundational knowledge claims about education, criticism is the attempt to apply the best human thought to test these foundations. Whether the research effort is directed at aptitude testing, behavior modification, organizational change, or instructional materials development, nothing of consequence follows if the research is faulty. A science is built upon its foundations, and confidence in the foundations is established through critical tests of them. Further, because research is open-ended, criticism can point to avenues of additional research needed to solidify the foundations of knowledge.

The second aim of criticism concerns policy-making and implementation. Policies are complex judgments, based partly upon facts and knowledge claims and partly upon values and value judgments. Policies are plans for action. To educate, to intervene in the lives of other human beings is a serious moral undertaking. If lack of knowledge is allowed to persist where knowledge could be obtained, the policy made and the action undertaken are grossly negligent of concern for the moral worth of other people. Criticism has a special role in policy analysis because it makes explicit this relation between knowledge and value found in educational policies.

The third aim of criticism concerns educational practice. In spite of rhetorical claims to the contrary, research has had little effect upon educational practice. Because research will often be conceived so as to change practice, criticism must obtain here too. Research to improve practice can lead to finding out facts, to discovering relations, to solving problems, to dispelling the comforting but misleading conventional wisdom which often stands in the way of establishing scientific knowledge. Criticism can be applied directly to the problems of justifying educational practice, but it joins research when it suggests the role of research in making practice more efficient, more effective, more humane, more insightful in its complex operation.

CRITICISM AND LITERARY CRITICISM

It is useful to borrow from the field of literary criticism a set of distinctions which apply to criticism of educational research. Literary critics distinguish four elements in criticism: the author (or artist), the work, the audience, and the universe. These distinctions are useful because importantly different criteria of assessment apply to different elements. For example, evaluating research can include checking the authority of the *author* and giving reasons for saying that the author or authors are experts in the area of research. Individuals with a history of high quality research justifiably deserve our attention because they have over the course of years earned the label of "expert." Experts are in a sense highly calibrated instruments; we trust their "readings," the points they make. Of course, any person is fallible; experts have their off day, busy people make mistakes, and so on. Nevertheless, experts continue to deserve the label as they continue to employ high standards for their work.

Many judges of research papers (editors of journals for example) make a practice of *not* knowing the author's name. This practice is one way to force attention to the *work* itself. Criteria of excellence commonly applied to individual works are very familiar: coherence of the reasoning from the problem statement to the conclusion, justification of the significance of the problem in the context in which it is placed, elegance of the design, choice of techniques of measurement, completeness of analysis, originality or novelty or creativity (breaking new ground), generation of new paradigms as well as connection to older paradigms to supply continuity with previous research.

Literary critics also judge the value of a work of art by the effects it has upon an appropriate *audience*; does it entertain, edify, point a moral, stimulate applause? Research products are also judged for their contribution to individuals who use the research products.

Does the set of knowledge claims of the research report stimulate consideration of educational change? There exists the balancing of judgment between research that is socially relevant, that solves or contributes to the solution of an immediate social problem, and research that furthers scientific knowledge, which at the time does not seem to have any social relevance. This comparison is sometimes referred to as the scientist riding a white charger (to change society) versus the scientist wearing his white coat (to contribute to scientific knowledge).

The fourth element of criticism is called "the universe." The term used for this element in these materials is the "phenomena of interest." We have in mind here the "stuff," the subject matter, the kind of thing the research is about. For example, in one of the studies in this book the authors are concerned with group productivity as it relates to group structure.

These phenomena are of considerable interest to school principals, industrial managers, and others. In this regard the research would be judged as potentially significant; potentially significant because the significance of such studies is not achieved by what it is about, but by what it tells us of what it is about. In other words, the phenomena of interest can be very important and the research relatively trivial if it fails to penetrate into the phenomena in any successful way.

As suggestive and fruitful as the model for criticism is that the literary critics use, it has some shortcomings as well. A chief shortcoming is the lack of attention to methods of work. This limitation is serious because the omnipresent focus of criticism found in contemporary educational research is precisely a concern with methods, with techniques of work, with research design, with statistical analysis.

OLD CHESTNUTS IN DISPUTE

Sometimes it is held that research is creative, that research generates new knowledge about the way the world works. On this ground research is distinguished from scholarship (sometimes called "library research") which only puts together or comments on knowledge which others have produced. In this sense, the products of criticism can be called "scholarship." Whatever the label agreed on, the relation between research and scholarship can be very close. Criticism which reveals faults in purported knowledge claims is both creative and valuable. Moreover, as indicated previously, both research and criticism (scholarship) require judgments about the same processes.

We have learned much from the college students who helped by using early drafts of these critical appraisals. One thing which many students reported inhibited their own appraisal was the lack of knowledge about statistics. We urge students, and other critics, to become knowledgeable about statistics, but we also recommend that one not be blinded by statistics. A kind of mindless reverence for numbers, tests of coefficients, F ratios and the like is to be avoided. One can still use judgment to see whether the data analyzed actually relate in a satisfactory way to the basic question, and how useful the data are in composing an answer. Any complex statistical analysis can be paraphrased in words, and the relations between variables can be interpreted in terms of the key concepts and the major knowledge claims. Research reports which rely on tests of statistical significance alone to establish educational significance are justifiably criticized.

Many people feel that the best way to criticize research is to compare the work against a checklist of possible faults. Many such checklists have been produced.[1] Checklists can be valuable, for they serve as a reminder of

---

[1] For a bibliography of such checklists, see Bruce B. Bartos, "A Review of Instruments Developed to Be Used in the Evaluation of the Adequacy of Reported Research." Bloomington, Indiana: Phi Delta Kappa, Research Service Center, Occasional Paper #2, 1969.

key features of an investigation which should be considered in any appraisal. Checklists, however, have at least two major shortcomings. First, they do not provide the criteria to judge the criteria. On what basis is the critic to decide if "the instruments are valid" or "the design appropriate"? Such judgments require knowledge of facts, concepts, and research paradigms. The model appraisals in this book are often very lengthy precisely because we have attempted not only to share our judgments but also to provide the basic information needed to reach such judgments. A second shortcoming of checklists is their almost total preoccupation with methods of work—i.e., with questions of research design, measurement, and analysis. The methods of work are very important of course, for they can make the difference between securing valid or invalid knowledge claims. But as researchers become more sophisticated about techniques and the number increases of those investigators capable of producing reasonably "tightly" designed research, it becomes increasingly important to ask an additional set of questions about the research—questions regarding its import for education and its implications for policy or practice. In the appraisals in this book, we have attempted not to slight these other dimensions of appraisal.

2

Eight Research Articles and Critiques: Description and Suggestions for Using Them

The assumption that repeated practice is required to learn to appraise educational research critically is implicit in the development of this book. Consequently, several research articles have been selected for appraisal. Before beginning this analysis task, the reader is urged to read carefully the following comments about the articles and the use of these materials.

DESCRIPTION

Characteristics used in selecting the eight articles reproduced in this book were problem area, methods of work, value, and difficulty.

PROBLEM AREA. A wide variety of educational topics is represented by the articles. A brief description of the primary problem area associated with each article is provided in Table 1. Several of the articles have abstracts which indicate more precisely the content of the research report.

METHODS. An attempt was made to select articles utilizing a diversity of approaches. In Table 1, brief labels are given for research types; but, as helpful as labels might be, they tend to mask the differences in methods employed by the several investigators.

VALUE. All the articles have redeeming features. It is true that we found much to criticize in each article, but any article can be criticized negatively. In our opinion, the articles are of reasonably good quality from which there is much to be learned.

DIFFICULTY. Results of the field testing of this book indicated that

Table 1
Summary of the Research Articles

Chapter	Senior Author	Problem Area	Type of Research
3	Charles H. Josephson	Grading and student attitudes	Description
4	Eleanor S. Kaplan	Evaluation of a Head Start program	Quasi-experimental
5	J. Richard Hackman	Prediction of "long-term" success	Prediction
6	Francis P. Hunkins	Effect of questioning procedures on student achievement	Experimental
7	Florence R. Harris	Reinforcement and behavioral modification	Case study/ experimental
8	David Elkind	Factors affecting the validity of creativity assessments	Experimental
9	Joanne R. Bronars	The case against experimenting with live animals in elementary school	Philosophical analysis
10	Edwin M. Bridges	Small group composition and productivity	Experimental

all articles were understandable to college students. Avoided were articles having sophisticated statistical analyses or dealing with topics requiring prior expertise in a specific content area to be understood. Several of the articles are accompanied by explanatory notes. Although there are some minor variations among them, all articles are moderately easy to understand.

The level of sophistication of the *critiques,* however, is not equal. In this respect, the articles are arranged in a crude ordering from simple to hard.

SUGGESTIONS FOR USE

The articles may be read in any order because each illustrates different concepts of research and these are not arranged sequentially. Nevertheless, it is probably wise to begin with one of the studies listed toward the top of Table 1 and work toward those which received a more intensive and sophisticated appraisal. Regardless of the article being analyzed, keep in mind the following points:

1. Any piece of research can be criticized negatively. The perfect study does not exist. Any investigator is operating within a system of constraints and must make compromises. The fact that weaknesses are evident in every study should not be taken to mean that they are without value. Quite the contrary. We consider each of the investigations in this book worthy of study.
2. The reader must be careful not to infer improperly that because the problem

area of a particular article is "irrelevant" to his specialty that the task of appraising the article is therefore irrelevant or valueless. The primary purpose of this book is to provide the reader with a set of generalizable skills. The specific articles are merely *vehicles* through which basic concepts can be taught and habits of workmanship practiced. Much is to be learned about the appraisal process regardless of the particular examples used for illustration.

3. The distinction between the research investigator and his work should be kept in mind. The reader should avoid taking sides for or against the investigator; avoid trying to be easy or hard on him. Rather, the task is to identify the strengths and weaknesses of the work itself and what these assessments mean for the educational value of the study and for the interpretations or knowledge claims resulting from the investigation.

4. The learner's expectation should *not* be to duplicate the model critique. This is frequently not appreciated by readers participating in field tryouts of the materials. Most readers are simply not able to appraise a study to the extent found in the model critiques. The model critiques are more complete and detailed than can be reasonably expected from even experienced researchers. The purpose of the model critiques is not to serve as the standard which students are expected to meet. Rather, they are complete and sometimes overblown statements designed in part to teach concepts and principles.

5. It is our intention that the materials be used either for group or individual instruction. In an effort to make the materials self-instructional, we have made heavy use of "student responses." Frequently these are representative replies of students participating in the field tryouts of the materials. These student responses are likely to be similar to comments that you may make. By providing our response to these statements, we hope to increase the interactiveness of the materials and their viability for self-instructional use.

6. The reader is expected to read carefully each article and then to appraise the work by responding to one or more questions. Many students who participated in the field tryout performed poorly on the appraisals because they failed either to read the article, the questions, or the appraisals carefully. We've heard much about programs designed to increase reading speed. In our opinion, people need to be instructed how to read more thoughtfully. The first principle in research criticism is to consider actively what one reads. The world needs more plodders!

7. One can simply read through these materials like a textbook and passively consider the appraisal tasks and model answers. Alternatively, the learner can write a response to each task, thus helping to insure his active involvement. We urge the latter. Appraising the work of others is a "doing" task just as performing research is. Neither performing nor criticizing research is easy; attention to detail is required, the work is demanding, the rewards are high.

3

Do Grades Stimulate Students to Failure?[*]

Charles H. Josephson

Nearly fifteen years ago Allison Davis took the position that students in slum schools may well find it more rewarding to be considered academic failures than to be successes in school.[1]

If false, this observation should not go unchallenged; if true, it should not be unheeded. The reason is simple: this observation washes away the underpinnings of one of the primary official sanctions traditionally used by the teacher and the school to direct pupil behavior.

All teachers offer promise of high grades as a reward for learning and promise of low grades as a punishment for failure. What irony there would be if we found a situation in which the teacher's reward has become the student's punishment—a situation in

which the student is actually motivated to "achieve" in the direction the teacher regards as "failure."

DO "GOOD" STUDENTS WANT TO FAIL?

To test the validity of Davis' observation, a study was conducted in a high school that serves one of Chicago's lower class neighborhoods. Although the group studied was small—only 106 students–and the classification as to level of ability of the students was relatively rough, the results of the study are surprising enough to merit serious consideration. The study began with the hypothesis that, if Davis' observation was true, the students most likely to succeed would feel the strongest pressure to fail. Thus, students of high ability would desire lower grades than students of low ability.

This inversion of values is not intuitively reasonable; we expect high-ability students to desire high grades and low-ability students to be quite

[*] Originally appeared in the Chicago Schools Journal, December 1961, pp. 122–127. Reprinted with permission. Published by Chicago State University.

[1] Allison Davis, Social Class Influences on Learning, The Inglis Lecture, Cambridge, Massachusetts, 1948. Pp. 29–30.

happy with low grades. But, for the following reasons, accepting Davis' observation leads logically to an inverse relationship of ability to grade aspirations.

To a large extent, adolescent behavior is peer-oriented; that is, among many forces that determine what the adolescent is likely to do must be included the desire to be accepted by his immediate circle of acquaintances. This involves accepting and following the common values of the group. For example, adolescent groups might include among these values such obvious peculiarities as a fondness for rock-and-roll music, a distinctive hair style, the ability or at least willingness to fight, and so forth.

COMPLIANCE WITH GROUP DEMANDS NOT CONSCIOUS FOR MAJORITY

However, one is likely to notice that a majority of the group do not *consciously* comply with group demands. In fact, the existence of such demands may be something of which most group members are not even aware; only those who are violating group values are likely to be conscious of the estrangement the violation brings. For example, if duck-tailed haircuts are highly regarded, only the group members who do not have duck-tails will feel a pressure to develop them. Those group members who have duck-tailed haircuts do not consciously recognize the existence of a pressure for them.

Now, Davis' observation suggests a peculiar value for adolescent groups from the lower classes, namely, low grades in school. The reasons for this—including among others a "natural" rebellion against authority—are far too complex to be included here. Yet if we accept this value as accurately depicting the state of affairs, it would follow that the student who has at one time received high grades will, on entering adolescence, discover that his high

grades are inhibiting peer acceptance. Thus, for the gifted student, high grades will come to be negatively perceived, while low grades develop a positive value. But the below-average student, whose low grades represent the summit of his achievement, will not even be aware of this value; in fact, he will wish that his intellectual efforts could be met with a higher reward. Thus he can accept the institutional value which favors high grades, perhaps reflecting his dreams of one day "getting smart," as one put it.

STUDENTS DIVIDED BY SCHOOL INTO THREE GROUPS

It is on this basis that we may hypothesize that in lower-class schools students of low ability will desire high grades, and students of high ability will desire low grades. The laborious task of defining what was included in the word "ability" was eliminated in this instance by assuming that the hierarchy of ability placement that was followed in the subject school was accurate. The school has three main ability groups: roughly 10 per cent of all students are placed in an "accelerated" program; about 50 per cent are in a "regular" plan; about 40 per cent are in a "remedial" program. Although teachers cite individual injustices, most agree that the general rankings are valid. That is, accelerated pupils have "more" ability than regular pupils, who in turn exceed the remedials.

One class was selected from each ability grouping. After a short introduction, primarily assuring that responses would be kept anonymous, four questions were asked:

(1) If you had your choice of any grade for this class, what grade would you select for yourself?

(2) If you could give an imaginary best friend the grade you think he would most like to receive, what grade would you give?

Table 1

Grade Desired	Remedial Class		Regular Class		Accelerated Class	
	Number of Students	Per Cent of Total	Number of Students	Per Cent of Total	Number of Students	Per Cent of Total
1........	11	33	8	23	12	31
2........	12	37	6	18	13	33
3........	9	27	14	41	12	31
4........	1	3	6	18	2	5
Totals	33		34		39	

(3) What grade do you feel you deserve in this course?

(4) What grade do you expect to receive in this course?

QUESTIONS DESIGNED TO INSURE HONESTY

The second question serves as an honesty check on the answer to the first question. One would assume an unwillingness to cooperate on the part of the student whose answer to these two questions differed appreciably. In only one case, in fact, did the response differ by more than one level. The last two questions were to assure that the assumption that achievement does not exceed aspirations would be reasonable for this group. This assumption was needed for certain implications.

The crucial question, of course, is the first. Answers to this question may be tabulated for the three groups, as follows (Per cents are in rounded figures, and grades are identified as "1" through "5," "1" being high and "5" indicating failure.) [see Table 1].

Even a cursory examination of the data presented for the three groups makes the conclusion inescapable that in the slightly more than one hundred pupils studied the direct inverse relationship between ability and grades desired does not obtain. However, additional study of the data reveals the possibility that ability groupings may have been made too fine. If regular and accelerated students are classified in a single category (average and above average), and if remedial students are treated as "below average," a significantly different picture emerges.

COMBINING HIGHER GROUPS PRODUCES DISTURBING PICTURE

Thirty-three per cent of the below average students select as most desirable the grade of "1" (the highest grade); only 27 per cent of the average and above average students select the highest grade. Thirty-seven per cent of the below average select grade "2"; only 26 per cent of the average and above average. Twenty-seven per cent of the below average select grade "3," 36 per cent of the average and above average select "3." Three per cent of the below average group choose grade "4," eleven per cent of the average and above average select the lowest grade offered. None of either group selects grade "5."

Even though such a liberal treatment of the data as this is required for the direct inverse relationship between grade aspirations and ability to become visible, there is cause for concern. Surprisingly, students in the sample obviously do not universally place a high value upon good grades. Moreover, students at and above the average in ability tend to prefer lower grades, as a group, than do students who are below average ability. In fact, note that only slightly more than half of the higher ability students would prefer to receive above average grades—assuming "3" to be the average. It is not surprising that no students select "5," the failing grade, as a desirable grade; this was expected. What is surprising is that, of the accelerated group of "gifted" students, only a third prefer superior grades; nearly the same number prefer average or below average grades.

GRADE ASPIRATIONS
REFLECT MOTIVATION

It is virtually axiomatic in psychological studies of learning that a student will learn primarily what he wants to learn. Hence we place great stress upon *motivation*, a term that suggests both the "amount of desire" a student possesses for learning a particular knowledge, and the process by which this "desire" may be brought into being or increased. Motivation is not well understood, but its importance under this definition is not disputed.

So far we have been talking about grade aspirations, not motivation. But it seems reasonable to suggest that aspirations, to a degree, reflect motivation; a student who desires a high grade will correspondingly adjust his efforts so that he will receive a grade as high as possible. And a student who envisions low grades as desirable will probably work to receive low grades. Thus, although aspirations do not *determine* achievement, we may be drawn to the conclusion that they nevertheless *limit* achievement.

What we are saying is that a student quite possibly will not achieve the grade he most desires, but he certainly will not achieve a grade higher than his aspirations. And the study bears this out. In only one case did a student feel he deserved or would receive a grade higher than the grade to which he aspired—a genuine over-achiever! In more than 75 per cent of the cases, the grade the student felt he deserved was the same or one point below his aspira-

tions. And in more than 65 per cent of the cases the grade the student actually expected to receive was identical with or one point below the grade aspiration.

RESULTS RAISE DOUBTS
ABOUT GRADING SYSTEM

These interpretations tend to dispute the value of a grading system such as the one followed by the school that was surveyed. This is not the first formal or informal dispute with grading as a means of pupil evaluation. Generally, the concern has been that grading is an inadequate and often an arbitrary means of measuring learning. (In fact, one study has shown that a similar value orientation on the part of teacher and student will tend to produce good grades more readily than will a student's acquisition of the body of knowledge the teacher presents.) Here, in addition, we seem able to conclude that grading as an evaluating process may actually serve as a deterrent to learning.

Currently, it appears that grading serves basically two functions: to evaluate learning, and to promote learning. As an evaluative tool, the letter grade says to the pupil, "You and your friends have been separated into five categories: you are most like category such-and-so." We need not be surprised or offended if the pupil selects friends of lesser ability and then seeks to join their grading category. As a means of promoting learning, the grade says to the pupil, "Here I am, now chase me!" It has been a dream of educators that all students, particularly the brightest ones, will "chase" the top grades. At least for the subject group, this is false. A specific grade indeed serves as a magnet, but it is not a magnet that draws the best out of the pupil. In fact, it may serve as a stimulus to failure for many students whose ability gives them no right to fail.

NO GOOD SUBSTITUTE
FOR GRADES AVAILABLE

Whether or not the two functions of evaluating and promoting learning make grades an appropriate tool for the teacher may, in the light of this, be open to question. In the years that have passed since Davis observed that we do not know how to properly reward students from lower classes, no widely accepted substitute for a system of grades has been developed. Grades as an administrative tool seem to be here to stay, and the day when a school's legal report will consist of a Certificate of Attendance rather than a grade awaits a utopia in which all students will learn according to their ability, reveling in the sheer joy of learning.

But in the meantime, even though the group sampled is quite small, one might consider two possible implications that can be derived from this study of grades and aspirations.

ABILITY GROUPING
MAY ENCOURAGE FAILURE

First: Ability grouping, as an administrative policy, may need to be reviewed. It is not far-fetched to suggest that many students wish to be moved from a higher "track" down to a lower one. Lighter work load, more congenial friends, and other reasons may account for this. Such a movement, it appears, should not be permitted; for if a student perceives any advantage that may be gained from failure, he will fail. If homogeneous groupings are indicated for a school, a final and irrevocable severing of intra-class relationships, by eliminating mobility between tracks, is suggested as the most effective deterrent to students who may be tempted to fail out of one track and into another. For grouping to be successful, we must assume our original placement to be correct, assume changes from track to track to be unnecessary, and, where failure

occurs, refuse to reward failure with the kind of transfer the student is seeking. Another aspect of ability grouping that might be reviewed is the grading system. To preclude any possibility of grade comparison among tracks, a distinctive grading system for each track is perhaps indicated.

Second: The peculiar construction of the data in the table above implies a direction for further research. This is a most tentative and blurred implication, requiring far more study and thought than has been applied.

AVERAGE STUDENTS HAVE
LOWEST ASPIRATION LEVEL

It seems uncontestable that a distinctively low-aspiration group emerges from these findings. It is not the low-ability group: Bless them, they'll go through life dreaming of the finest and saying, "Maybe, if only I'd worked a little harder. . . ." And it's not the high-ability group: Their aspirations, if a bit underwhelming, at least tend to concentrate above the average. But how about the middle group: the *ordinary* student of *normal* ability who is studying at the *usual* pace in a *regular* class? Observe the data: His aspirations are so dulled that, in general, he is content with average or below average grades! Could it be that we who are in education have spent so much time, energy, and effort studying the special groups of students with easily identified peculiarities—the slow reader, the musically gifted, the math whiz, the foreign language non-learner, the social studies misfit, the physically handicapped, *ad infinitum*—that we have missed the gargantuan middle group of the mass of students? Because we have been blind to them as individuals, have we caused a degeneration of aspiration? All is not necessarily well with the masses. We need some research aimed at stimulating the aspirations of the ordinary, average, normal student.

But administrative policy or research study does not implement a solution. The teacher is crucial; he must recognize the problem. And the solution must eventually come through the teacher, if it comes.

In some parts of this and other countries, dog racing is a popular sport. At dog races, a mechanical rabbit runs around the track ahead of the field of dogs. Occasionally one of the racing dogs gets tired of chasing the ordinary mechanical rabbit, and refuses to budge. In such a situation, however, the dog owner does not throw away the dog; he rather searches out a new kind of rabbit—changes its color or size, or gives the dog some other excuse for running. This study suggests that in slum schools our dogs are not chasing our rabbits. Perhaps what we need is a new kind of rabbit!

CRITIQUE

1. QUESTION:

In study after study, all too often the problem which occasioned the research, and which is used to introduce the research report, turns out not to be the problem actually dealt with by the study as conducted. We are reminded of a cartoon in which a very young boy asks a girl if she can come out and play. The girl responds that she is younger than the boy. The puzzled boy turns to the reader and asks whether the girl's response has answered his question.

The mismatch between problem statement and answers collected by the investigator is seldom as gross as that confronted by the boy. Nonetheless, a good critic must be alert for such incongruity. He may ask: Do the data provide evidence about the stated problem? Given the data actually collected what question could be composed to which the data would be an answer? Have the phenomena of interest shifted as the study progressed? What conclusions and interpretations is the investigator entitled to draw from the findings?

Five possible problem statements about which data could have been collected are listed in this first question. We are asking you to practice an important skill—namely relating data to the question posed. One does not really know what the problem is until the solution emerges. Another way of stating this point is to say that any question will remain ambiguous until data which count as the answer to the question are specified.

Consider the following statements:

A. "Grades stimulate students to failure."
B. "Students in slum schools find it more rewarding to be considered academic failures than successes."
C. Students "most likely to succeed" feel the strongest pressure to fail.

D. "... in lower-class schools students of low ability will desire high grades, and students of high ability will desire low grades."

E. "There is a discrepancy between aspiration and achievement."

Which one of the preceding options most accurately reflects the problem statement that the data of this paper deal with? Why? Give reasons for rejecting *each* of the other items. (*Note*: We are NOT asking you which statement is true. We are asking you to indicate which statement represents a hypothesis the investigator attempted to test empirically, i.e., the hypothesis about which the investigator collected data.)

1. ANSWER:

A. Answer A is quoted from the title. Titles of articles are almost always both illuminating and misleading. Except in the most technical journals, titles are phrased in ordinary language and it is difficult to achieve precise meaning with the looseness and ambiguity of ordinary language.[1] Note ambiguities in a key word of this title, "failure." To fail can have three meanings: (a) to fail in school (as a dropout, perhaps); (b) to get a failing grade in a single course (as "to fail algebra"); (c) to fail to achieve at a level commensurate with ability (to underachieve).

For the three reasons which follow, option *A* was not considered the best statement of the question to which the data reported in the study are relevant. First, the word "stimulate" suggests a causal connection and no such relationship between grades and failure was established. Further, the actual grades students receive are not given, and thus we have no data about failure in the sense of a teacher giving a pupil a failing grade. Finally, the data which are gathered pertain to a slum school and the students in several tracks, and these facts are not mentioned in option A.

B.   Option B is Allison Davis's position but Josephson did not actually collect data on what is *rewarding* to students. Nevertheless, some support for this position would be the finding that of 106 students interviewed in the slum school, a large number aspire to (i.e., would "select") grade 5, the failing grade. However, not one student gave that response, and the investigator essentially ignored this fact. One might go one step further to ask if the data presented by this investigator actually could be interpreted as falsifying Davis's position as stated in option *B*. The answer is "yes," if one can establish that what is rewarding to students and what they would "select" are identical.

C.   Although the investigator states option *C* as a beginning hypothesis (paragraph 4), he gathered no data on pressure; he thus cannot relate pressure to fail to a measure of likelihood of success.

D.   We think this choice is the most accurate one. See the first paragraph in the section entitled "Students Divided by School into Three Groups" where the hypothesis is explicitly stated. Note also that the table giving the data closely follows the hypothesis. Recall that in question 1 we asked if the hypothesis was tested in this study and not whether it could be considered true on other grounds.

E.   Although we have data on an *expectation* of achievement, we have no data on achievement itself and therefore cannot compare achievement to aspiration. The three tracks are said to represent ability levels. If they are also viewed as defining an achievement variable, then some gross data on the discrepancy between aspiration and achievement are provided and option *E* could be considered an acceptable (but probably not the best) answer.

---

[1] For a further discussion hear Robert M. W. Travers, "The Limitations of Variables Derived from Common Language" (Washington, D.C.: American Educational Research Association, Cassette Tape Series 10B, 1971).

2. QUESTION:

After considering the real purpose of this study, cite one very important reason why research on the broad question addressed in this paper is of value.

2. ANSWER:

The reward system of a slum school is being studied. There are several acceptable reasons you might have given to explain why research on this topic is of value. One that appeals to us is that IF the research should point up the fact that the grading system is not working as intended, that "the teacher's reward has become the student's punishment," or that the extrinsic rewards (for example, the grades) of the system wield such a powerful influence that the intrinsic rewards of learning are diminished or bypassed, THEN such distortion would provide support for changing present educational policies and practices. The primary aim of an educational system should be its true educational goals and not the external trappings attached to these goals. Florence Nightingale once said of hospitals that at least they should not spread disease; school systems should at least not discourage true learning.

3. QUESTION:

Refer to the table presented in the article and to the investigator's descriptive labels for the grade categories in the section entitled, "Combining Higher Groups Produces Disturbing Picture." Which one(s) of the following statements is (are) a factually correct interpretation(s) of the findings for students in the accelerated class?

A. Only 1/3 prefer superior grades; nearly the same number prefer average or below average grades.
B. About 2/3 prefer grades above average; only two students preferred below average grades.

How do statements A and B differ in the impression they give?

3. ANSWER:

Both statements are technically correct given the investigator's interpretation that 1 means superior and 3 means average. They differ in the impression they give the reader. The A statement suggests failure of the school to keep high the aspirations of good students. The B statement suggests most students in accelerated classes want good grades. The A statement is the way this investigator interprets the findings (see last sentence in second paragraph of "Combining Higher Groups Produces Disturbing Picture"). We think it acceptable for a researcher to try to find what his reasoning leads him to expect. He should not, however, stop at this point but should examine alternative explanations. We must remember that one can say a cup is half full or half empty and be correct in both instances. A researcher should be able to, and further has an obligation to, say both, realizing the different possible impressions he may give his readers from these different viewpoints.

4. QUESTION:

Note that from each of the three programs (remedial, regular, accelerated) one class was selected in some unspecified fashion (see paragraph two, "Students Divided by School into Three Groups."). Alternatively, the investigator could have selected the required number of students randomly from all the students enrolled in each of the programs. We believe this latter selection plan to be far superior. Why?

4. ANSWER:

The investigator wishes to compare the grade students of different ability levels desire. Because he selected only one class from each program, he cannot distinguish differences due to program/ability level from those due to classroom influences. We know from other research that on many variables classrooms differ markedly from one another even when the classrooms are composed of students of the same general ability. The particular teacher, classroom peer relations, and other factors can lead to a distinctive kind of response from students in a particular classroom. The responses of pupils from one of the classes might not be typical of those from other classes in the same track. Thus the differences the investigator notes in the data shown in the table on page 11 may not be due to program/ability level group differences at all but to other attributes of the three particular classrooms he selected for the study. Had a random sampling procedure been used, students from *several classrooms within each program* would have been selected and this source of confusion in data interpretation would have been avoided.

5. QUESTION:

Recall that when the students were divided into the three programs (accelerated, regular, remedial) and their desired grades noted (see data in the table on page 11) the investigator concludes that the expected, ". . . inverse relationship between ability and grades desired does not obtain." However, when the investigator reclassifies the regular and accelerated students into a single category, ". . . a significantly different picture emerges." Is it wrong for an investigator to manipulate his data in this way in search of confirming evidence? Why?

5. ANSWER:

We don't think so, provided the cautions mentioned in the next paragraph are noted. Such "teasing" of the data in which after-the-fact hypotheses are tested can provide insights. Such unplanned analyses, however, are generally more valuable as possible leads for future research than as firm conclusions.

We suggest these cautions. First, the data should be presented in the manner the investigator expected to present them before they were collected (the present investigator does this), or else the departure should be explained. Second, the investigator should state or imply (as the present investigator does) that the particular analysis presented was suggested to him only after the data were observed. Third, the investigator should also report plausible after-the-fact analyses which do not support his expected conclusions. In this regard, it is of interest to note that in this study the largest group differences occur when the extreme groups, the remedial and accelerated classes, are compared to the regular classes. This finding, if replicated by others, would suggest a much different interpretation from that provided by the investigator. Finally, relationships found as a result of such after-the-fact manipulating must not be taken too seriously, especially those: (a) not predicted ahead of time; (b) not amenable to a reasonable interpretation; (c) based on a small number of observations and thus more likely to be unstable and not replicable; and (d) emerging from a large number of comparisons. When enough things are examined, some comparisons will seem "significant" by chance alone.

6. QUESTION:

Both in the case where the data for the three programs (ability level groupings) are kept separate, and in the case where the data for the regular and accelerated classes are combined, the differences among programs in the percent of students desiring the various grades are *not statistically significant* according to our calculations. What is the importance of this statement?

6. ANSWER:

Lack of statistical significance means that the differences among the percentages in the three columns in the table in the article could be due not to differences between program/ability level groups in the grades desired, but simply to errors in sampling. Failure to get statistical significance can be interpreted as a vote of no confidence that the differences which were found will be observed with another sample of students. The investigator should have realized that the group differences in grade preferences should not have been taken seriously and therefore he should have refrained from such strong language as, "It seems uncontestable that a distinctively low-aspiration group (i.e., the middle group) emerges from these findings." (See concluding section of the article.)

7. QUESTION:

Although there are serious flaws in this study, there are also some commendable aspects. List four such positive features (not conclusions) of this paper.

7. ANSWER:

The following list is meant to be suggestive and not necessarily complete.

a) The investigator sees research as having a clear bearing on educational policy and practice, and suggests changes in these practices based on such relevant research.

b) He uses his reasoning powers in the search for an explanation of phenomena he thought he observed in the schools.

c) Even though a teacher in the schools at the time of the study, he does a study— collects the data *in situ*—which makes good use of an educationally relevant context.

d) The investigator cites a puzzling observation in the literature (Allison Davis's position) which is an impetus to research.

e) The investigator realizes some of the inadequacies of his study and that more complete and better planned studies need to be made.

f) He published locally where the impact of such a controversial study will most likely have an effect.

g) The investigator attempted to obtain valid measures of aspirations. He thought of devices (e.g., anonymous responses and additional questions) as an "honesty check" to the first question. We do not claim he was successful, but we do commend the attempt.

h) He manipulated his data in more than one way. (See question and answer 5.)

i) The research was open-ended in the sense that it suggested further investigation.

j) The paper was highly readable and written in an interesting fashion.

Concluding Remark:

In their classic paper, Campbell and Stanley wrote:

> At present, there seem to be two main types of "experimentation" going on within schools: 1) research "imposed" upon the school by an outsider, who has his own ax to grind and whose goal is not immediate action (change) by the school; and 2) the so-called "action" researcher, who tries to get teachers themselves to be "experimenters", using that word quite loosely. The first researcher gets results that may be rigorous but not applicable. The latter gets results that may be highly applicable but probably not "true" because of extreme lack of rigor in the research.[2]

The present paper clearly falls into the second category.

---

[2] Donald T. Campbell and Julian C. Stanley, *Experimental and Quasi-experimental Designs for Research* (Skokie, Ill.: Rand McNally, 1966), p. 21.

4

"Head Start" Experience and the Development of Skills and Abilities in Kindergarten Children[*1]

Eleanor S. Kaplan

Critics' Note:

> *The present article would be classified as an example of educational evaluation. There is disagreement among experts regarding the distinction between* evaluation *and* research. *Some say that the purpose of evaluation is to derive assessments of the worth of particular instances of educational undertakings such as individual textbooks and specific programs; the purpose of research is to produce generalizable conclusions. We see the distinction primarily to be one of purpose rather than procedure. In both studies we ask whether the activities followed permitted the investigator to accomplish the objectives of the study.*

INTRODUCTION

Project Head Start, a federal program under the supervision of the Office of Economic Opportunity, was introduced in the summer of 1965. This project was developed as a result of the urgent interest in a national program to prepare economically and socially disad-

vantaged children for kindergarten. In New York City, more than eighteen thousand youngsters participated in this pre-kindergarten program.

The purpose of this study was to evaluate whether the children who participated in Project Head Start were better prepared for kindergarten than those who did not participate, with particular reference to verbal communication abilities, visual discrimination and naming abilities, and certain motor coordination skills.

There is a strong and growing movement to establish pre-schools of this nature for socially and economical-

* *Originally appeared in* Graduate Research in Education and Related Disciplines, *April 1966, pp. 4–28.*
[1] This study was carried out under the supervision of Judith Greenberg and David J. Fox.

ly deprived children who are four and five years of age. It is felt that the formation of pre-schools will provide these children with challenge, enrichment, and a desire to learn in school. As a consequence of this type of compensatory program, it is hoped that eventually some of the potential deficiencies resulting from the environment in which these children live, can be overcome.

Compared with children from more privileged environments, children from marginal social and economic circumstances frequently enter school with poorer preparation for the demands of the learning processes and the behavioral requirements of the classroom. For these children, vital aspects of growing and learning are not provided by the home and must therefore be provided through some other medium such as the school. (Brunner, 1964)

In order to counteract some of the poor effects of a culturally disadvantaged environment on school performance, it is necessary to provide enrichment and training in the skills and abilities underlying success in the classroom. The pre-kindergarten age of about four or five years is now considered the opportune time to begin striving toward these goals.

Review of the Literature

The concern with the socially and culturally disadvantaged as a specific educational problem is relatively recent. This interest has been fostered by the increasing urbanization of our population and by the awareness of stratification and differential privilege within our society. Riessman (1962) says that cultural deprivation is used interchangeably with educational deprivation to refer to the limited access to education on the part of the lower socioeconomic groups. This is the sense in which the term will be employed in this study. Henry (1963) pointed out that the middle-class home contains a "hidden curriculum" which enables the

child to deal appropriately with his first school experience. The disadvantaged home contains no such curriculum and, as pointed out by Deutsch (1964, 1965a), is discontinuous with the school environment.

Passow (1963) asserted that the deficiencies of the children from disadvantaged circumstances can be overcome by proper educational planning. He emphasized the importance of early compensation for the deficiencies in the home environment. Riessman (1962) argued, however, that educational programs for the disadvantaged can be begun at any age. Such programs, according to Riessman (1964), should consider the strengths that disadvantaged children possess in nonverbal communication and independence, and that they should not rely on the middle-class model. However, Riessman's argument on cultural relativism does not take into consideration the increasing industrialization of our society and the greater dependence in such a society on verbal communication, which entails the need for facility in verbal skills such as reading and writing.

John (1963) examined certain patterns of linguistic and cognitive behavior in samples of Negro children and reported that consistent class differences in language skills were shown to emerge between groups of Negro children of different socio-economic classes. Middle-class children from more advantaged environments were reported to have a better command of language in terms of its classificatory and problem-solving functions. Middle-class Negro children surpassed their lower-class agemates in possessing a larger vocabulary (WISC Vocabulary results) and a higher non-verbal intelligence quotient (Lorge-Thorndike IQ Test) in their ability to produce a best-fit response. The middle-class child had an advantage over the lower-class child in tasks requiring precise and somewhat abstract language due to the amount of help available to him in his home. The acquisition of more abstract and integrative language seemed to be hampered by the living conditions in the homes of the lower-class children. The educational implications of these findings point to the need for greater emphasis on language teaching for disadvantaged children. In studying different verbal learning tasks, Jensen (1963) found that paired-associate learning involved greater reliance on verbal mediations than did serial learning. According to John (1963) and Bernstein (1960, 1962), the socially disadvantaged were less facile in the use of verbal mediators. The above studies elucidate the educational problems involved in attempting to reverse the effects of environmental linguistic deprivation. (Kendler, 1963)

According to the formulation of Bernstein (1960), the cumulative deficiency in language functioning results from the failure in development through the years of an elaborated language system with accurate grammatical order and logical modifiers, mediated through a grammatically complex sentence structure, containing prepositions, impersonal pronouns, and a discriminative selection of adjectives and adverbs. Bernstein (1960) asserts that lower-class speech is characterized by simple, unfinished sentences and a rigid, limited use of adjectives and adverbs. He also evaluated the complexity of sentences (simple or complex) and the percentage of adjectives and adverbs of the total words spoken by the subjects during the verbal part of the test. The usage of adjectives and adverbs is the start of a more complex type of verbal communication. Two related studies (C. P. Deutsch, 1964; John & Goldstein, 1964) indicated that lower-class deprived homes are deficient in the stimulation required for adequte development of discrimination and of language skills.

Montague (1964) tested kindergarten children on arithmetic concepts and showed that those from high so-cio-economic areas scored significantly higher on the inventory than those from low socio-economic areas. This tends to confirm the view of Deutsch (1962, p. 8) that:

> A child from any circumstance who has been deprived of a substantial portion of the variety of stimuli which he is maturationally capable of responding to is likely to be deficient in both the formal and contentual equipment required for learning.

The major emphasis in educational programming for disadvantaged children has been to initiate programs before the gap between these children and their more advantaged peers widens beyond reach. This emphasis has led to the development of programs on the nursery or pre-school level. Nursery schools have been expanding since the beginning of the twentieth century. There were three nursery schools in the United States in 1918 and by 1931 the number had grown to five hundred. Private nursery schools and experimental schools connected to universities have been popular with the more privileged groups. Nursery schools for the poor were encouraged and financially supported by the federal government during the depression under President Franklin Delano Roosevelt. In 1933 some 2,400 nursery school programs were in operation in the United States, most of them supported by the WPA. During World War II the federal government put its support behind nursery schools, known then as Child Care Centers, where working mothers could leave their preschool-age children. In the past few years a great emphasis has been placed on preschool education for the culturally deprived.

The usefulness of preschool programs that are oriented toward the stimulation of cognitive development found general support in Fowler (1962) and in Jensen (1963). The psychological basis for such programs was specifically elaborated by Hunt (1964) and their usefulness explicitly upheld by Deutsch (1964b). Hunt (1964) examined evidence which refuted the concepts of fixed intelligence and predetermined development. It is experience, he argued, particularly experience that comes before the advent of language, that is important. He regards the effects of cultural deprivation as analogous to the effects of experimental deprivation in infancy and early childhood. He indicated that appropriately organized cognitive stimulation during the preschool years can be highly effective in accelerating the development of intellectual functions. He recommended a curriculum that is consistent with children's environmental experiences and their initial abilities and disabilities. Hunt (1964) also cited evidence in support of programs for preschool enrichment for culturally deprived children and asserted that such children are poorly prepared to meet the demands of the school and that initial failures are almost inevitable. Hunt assumed that the culture of the lower-class environment is different from the culture that has molded the school and its educational theory and this idea is also supported by Riessman (1962).

Deutsch (1965a) felt that the goal of a preschool program for disadvantaged children should be:

> . . . to stimulate in young children the skills that underlie school performance and which according to both research findings and practical school experience are evidently not stimulated by disadvantaged backgrounds and poor environments. A broader goal is to help each child to realize more fully his own productive potential for his own good and for the good of society. (p. 51)

Current preschool programs for the culturally disadvantaged proceed on the assumption that the deprived child's academic deficit increases as he moves through the grades. (Stine, 1965) An early school program is needed to head off the cumulative deficiency and to attempt to neutralize cultural deprivation before school entrance. The early school admission of children from depressed areas should specifically aid language development and abstract thinking. It should provide a pleasurable emotional experience and new opportunity for the development of social and intellectual ability. (Stine, 1965) However, it is generally recognized that early intervention by the school is not likely to succeed if it is not accompanied by reinforcement and support in the home. Parents should be brought into such programs at the beginning as partners in the educational enterprise. Their resources for serving in this capacity are much greater than is generally realized. (Haskell, 1965)

Spurred by Ford Foundation grants and the Johnson Administration's War on Poverty, preschool education programs for culturally deprived children are moving along on a statewide basis in Pennsylvania, as well as in four eastern cities, New York, New Haven, Baltimore and Boston. Each program is developing its own methods of introducing educationally underprivileged children to experiences and thinking patterns that will help them start school on a par with other students. Although the goals of the plans are similar, each program has developed in its own way. Similar preschool projects for culturally deprived children are currently underway in many cities throughout the nation but progress reports are not yet available.

Project Head Start was introduced in the summer of 1965 on an experimental basis by the U.S. Office of Economic Opportunity to provide preschool learning experiences for deprived children who otherwise would not be exposed to such benefits. The program has already benefitted some 560,000 youngsters in 2,500 communities in the United States. Reference can be made to only a few of the many Head Start centers as there are only thirty-five children in this study.

There have been various criticisms made about the Head Start Project; the program was very expensive (it cost about $112,000,000) and it was insufficiently prepared and rushed through. There was inadequate provision for evaluation and follow-up. Many experts have complained that Head Start lacked the kind of experimental preparation such as pre-testing and careful study of the selected population. Thus far, the official reports are only based on a small sample of the children in certain centers and are unscientific and sketchy. (Hechinger, 1965b) In addition, there were no criteria established to judge the effectiveness or preparedness of the teachers in the project. Deutsch (Hechinger, 1965b) said that many of the programs lacked the necessary preparedness and certain others were purely custodial. It has been pointed out that compensatory education for children of deprived minorities is no substitute for changes in the structure of education itself. (Hechinger, 1965; Riessman, 1962) It is of little use to give minority group children an opportunity to begin slightly ahead of the class, if, at the same time, their regular schooling is not made relevant to them. The school itself must continue to develop the parent participation fostered in Head Start. (Hechinger, 1965a)

Prior educational research has shown that early compensatory education is of very limited, short-term benefit unless there is a consistent follow-up. If children's gains are not constantly reinforced through the years, they disappear within a few years. Dr. Edmund W. Gordon, Head Start's director of research said: "It is vital that the summer crash program not be regarded as a substitute for the regular and continuing education of disadvantaged children." (Hechinger, 1965b, p. 75) An inherent danger of the project is that it may deceive the public into believing that ear-

ly success can be easily translated into later success without the investment of money, time, and personnel on a continuous basis. This painful lesson has been demonstrated by the initial success but long-term failure of New York City's Higher Horizons Program. (Hechinger, 1965b)

Although it is too early to evaluate the long-term success of the preschool programs for disadvantaged children because they are very recent undertakings, some of the immediate effects can be evaluated. Gang, a principal of a Harlem elementary school has, for instance, reported that many teachers in his school have found better school adjustment among the Head Start children as compared to children who did not participate in the program. (Hechinger, 1965b)

Project Head Start has received the approval of the United Parents Association in New York City. Although it cautioned against making premature educational judgments about the Head Start program, the UPA commended the break-through made in reaching the hitherto hard-to-reach parents of disadvantaged children. The UPA, through its visits to the child centers, found that although the staff of teachers, aides, and volunteers was adequate, some of the physical plants were not. A report issued to the New York City Board of Education by the UPA recommended more adequate planning for future preschool projects, establishment of a liaison between the winter and summer staff, and smaller classes in all early childhood programs. (Emery, 1965)

One of the main goals of Project Head Start was to develop speech and verbal communication through "show and tell," listening to sounds, discrimination between sounds, using names to individuate, and listening to records and tape recordings. (Graham & Hess, 1965) For the purposes of this investigation, verbal communication will be operationally defined in this study as verbal fluency, enunciation, verbal usage, ability to structure sentences, and story-telling ability.

A second goal was to develop the visual and observational abilities of the children by having them become familiar with the letters of the alphabet, classify objects, become aware of the environment, combine awareness of environment with learning similarities and differences, reading pictures, and distinguishing colors and shapes. (Graham & Hess, 1965) Visual discrimination and naming abilities will be operationally defined as ability to discriminate and name various colors and shapes. Demonstrations were used in Head Start to help teach the motor coordination skills such as buttoning, cutting, and coloring with crayons. (Graham & Hess, 1965) Throughout this study, motor coordination skills were interpreted as skill in cutting, buttoning one's clothes, coloring, and drawing the figure of a man. Other goals of the Head Start program were to develop a sense of self, develop creativity, self-expression, and curiosity through science.

The present study was designed to compare children who had participated in Project Head Start with children who had not participated in the project in order to assess the immediate benefits of this experience.

Hypotheses

Kindergarten children who participated in Project Head Start will be superior to a matched group of children who did not participate in Project Head Start in:

1. Verbal communication abilities, as measured by:
   a) verbal fluency
   b) enunciation
   c) ability to structure sentences
   d) story-telling ability
   e) verbal usage.
2. Visual discrimination and naming abilities, as measured by:

a) naming colors
b) naming of shapes.
3. Motor coordination skills, as measured by:
   a) drawing figures
   b) coloring
   c) cutting
   d) buttoning their clothing.

PROCEDURE

This study was conducted in a public elementary school in a lower-class neighborhood. The school provides special services such as additional reading teachers, guidance counselors, non-English coordinators, and instructional materials designed to accelerate the achievement of children of low socio-economic background who are limited in their development by environmental factors beyond their control.

Sample

The subjects selected for this study were seventy disadvantaged kindergarten children between the ages of four years eight months and five years six months. The experimental group consisted of thirty-five children who had participated in Project Head Start during the previous summer. The control group consisted of thirty-five children with no preschool experience.

Individual children in the control group and the experimental group were matched on the following criteria:

1. Sex: Each pair consisted of two members of the same sex. There were fourteen girls and twenty-one boys in each group.
2. Ethnic Background: Each pair consisted of two members of the same race. There were seventeen Negro and eighteen Puerto Rican children in each group.
3. Age: The maximum difference in ages for the members of a pair was four months.
4. Language in the home: Each pair

consisted of two members in whose homes the same languages were spoken.

5. Age of siblings: The ages of the siblings of the matched pairs were similar.

The socio-economic status of the families of the subjects was approximately the same. It was assumed that the factors of sex, ethnic background, age, language spoken in the home, and age of siblings provided an accurate method of matching the two groups of kindergarten children in this study.

Techniques of Measurement

A "Describe This Picture Test" was designed by the researcher to determine verbal communication abilities. The test, which was given to each child individually, consisted of a picture of two firetrucks going to a fire, two policemen stopping traffic, people watching, and a dog running behind the trucks. The children were asked to: "Tell me everything that you see in this picture." Subsequently, each subject was told: "Tell me a story about this picture." Testing was stopped when each subject insisted that he had nothing more to say.

The subjects were graded on their verbal abilities in terms of their ability to tell a story, ability to structure sentences, verbal fluency, verbal usage, and enunciation. Ability to tell a story was rated according to the complexity of statements about the picture. For purposes of computation a numerical value of zero was assigned if nothing was said; a value of one was assigned if the picture was described; a value of two was assigned if the picture was described with considerable detail; a value of three was assigned if an unorganized story was told; a value of four was assigned if an organized creative story was told.

The ability of the subjects to structure sentences was rated as follows: a value of zero was assigned if nothing was said; a value of one if phrases were used; a value of two if the subject used simple sentences; a value of three if the subject used complex sentences.

Verbal fluency was measured by the total number of words employed in describing and telling a story about the picture. The verbal usage score was the percentage of adjectives and adverbs of the total number of words used by the subject.

The enunciation ability of the subject was rated by assigning a score of one to enunciation which was fairly clear and a score of two to enunciation which was very clear.

Specific instruments devised by the investigator were used to measure certain visual discrimination and naming abilities which had been developed in the Project Head Start. Each subject was given an individual oral test to measure his grasp of color concepts. This test consisted of showing each child four shapes colored red, blue, yellow, and green and then asking the child to name each color. One point was given for each color named correctly.

Three of these shapes were used again in a similar procedure to test the subjects' ability to identify the shapes of a circle, a square, and a triangle. If the child named some object that resembled the shape, the child's exact words were recorded. One point was given for each shape named correctly and one-half point was given for each object similar to the shape named, if the name of shape was not stated.

In order to evaluate motor coordination skills each child was asked to draw a picture of a man, and it was rated using norms set up in the Goodenough-Draw-A-Man Test for Negro Elementary School children. This rating scale was used as a measure of drawing skill and not as a measure of intelligence, as it is commonly used. The possibility that intelligence quotients were raised by participation in Project Head Start was not evaluated in this study.

In order to test cutting and coloring skills, subjects were each given a simple outline of a squirrel and told to color and cut it out with a scissors. The subjects had previously seen pictures of squirrels and had discussed them. The completed productions were rated according to how well the child was able to follow the squirrel outline in cutting and also the type of stroke used in coloring with crayons. The rating scale for both skills was as follows: poor was assigned a numerical value of one; fair a value of two; good a value of three; very good a value of four; excellent a value of five.

An observational technique was used to evaluate the subjects' ability to button their own coats or sweaters. Every day before the children left school they lined up before the investigator who observed which children were able to button their own clothing and which children could not perform this task. Those who stated that they could not button their own clothing were urged to try in order to eliminate the possibility that they merely desired the adult's attention. A score of one was given if the subject was able to button his own coat and a score of zero was given if he could not.

Former Project Head Start students were identified from their cumulative record cards. The admission forms of all the students provided information on sex, date of birth, race, age, number of siblings, and languages spoken in the home. These data were used to match the students. All of the instruments designed to test the visual discrimination abilities and motor coordination skills were presented to the children at the beginning of kindergarten in order to insure that these skills and abilities to be tested were not learned during the kindergarten experience.

Both verbal communication ability tests and visual discrimination ability tests were presented to each subject individually in a quiet room where a ta-

ble and two chairs had previously been arranged. Each subject was allowed as much time as he needed to answer each question and was reminded of the directions at short intervals. He was permitted to change his mind (if he wanted to) and was asked to guess if he was unsure. The subject was not told whether he was right or wrong but was encouraged throughout the testing procedure. After each question was answered, he was told that he had done very well.

The children's performance was evaluated, according to specific criteria, by the investigator and an additional rater who had also been working with these subjects. The investigator had done the original classification of the experimental and control groups, but made no effort to remember who was in each group during the study. The other rater had no knowledge at any time of the names of the subjects in each classification. Each scorer worked independently without knowledge of the scores assigned by the other. The results showed very close rater agreement. In the few instances where large differences occurred, each rater re-evaluated his scoring individually. One limitation of this study was that the researcher may have been unconsciously aware of the group classification of some of the children and this may have influenced some of the scoring of the skills and abilities of the subjects.

A second limitation of this study was that it was not possible to test the children in the skills and abilities investigated herein prior to their attendance in Project Head Start. It is possible that the two groups differed on the various abilities before the Head Start program began.

Analysis of the Data

The median score on each test was obtained for each group and used to compare the performance of the two groups. The over-all median of each test was obtained from the combined test scores of all seventy subjects in order to dichotomize the groups on test performance. Eleven chi-square tests using these medians were performed and the .05 level of significance chosen as the critical value.

than 5%) and thus the chance-alone hypotheses is not very plausible, the investigator indicates that the difference was statistically significant and, presumably, the Head Start program had an effect.

CRITICS' NOTE:

For each set of data the investigator conducted a chi-square test of the statistical significance of the difference between the score distribution found for the two groups of children. The investigator was seeking to determine whether the difference in the proportion of students in the two groups who are above a particular score could happen by chance alone. Specifically, the statistical test indicates the probability of getting such a large difference in proportions if only chance (i.e., sampling variability) were operating. When this probability is small (defined in this paper as less

RESULTS

Verbal Communication Abilities

It was hypothesized that kindergarten children who participated in Project Head Start would be superior in the following verbal communication abilities: (a) ability in telling a story; (b) ability to structure sentences; (c) verbal fluency; (d) verbal usage; (e) enunciation.

Table 1 shows the story-telling ratings for children in the Head Start and non-Head Start groups. The median rating for the Head Start group was 3.3 and for the non-Head Start group, 2.3. The median for the combined

Table 1
Verbal Ability: Telling a Story

Story-telling Rating	Number of Children Receiving Each Rating	
	Head Start (35)	Non-Head Start (35)
4	10	4
3	11	7
2	6	10
1	7	11
0	1	3
	Median = 3.3	Median = 2.3

Table 2
Ability to Structure Sentences

Scale Rating for Sentence Structure Used	Number of Children Receiving Each Rating	
	Head Start (35)	Non-Head Start (35)
3	22	11
2	9	14
1	3	5
0	1	5
	Median = 3.2	Median = 2.5

group was 2.8. Using 3 and above as the upper category, the chi-square median test ($\chi^2 = 5.74$) was statistically significant (p < .025), indicating that the children in the Head Start group showed greater ability in telling a story.

Table 2 presents the ratings of the students' ability to structure sentences. The median of the Head Start group was 3.2 compared to 2.5 for the non-Head Start group. The median for the combined groups was 2.9. Using 3 as the upper category, the chi-square median test in effect compared children who gave complex sentences with those who did not. The chi-square value of 6.94 was statistically significant.

cant (p < .01). The Head Start group thus excelled the non-Head Start group in the ability to speak in complex sentences.

Table 3 presents the results of the verbal fluency test. The number of words used by the subjects on the "Describe This Picture" test ranged from 0 through 270. The median of the Head Start group was 96 and the non-Head Start group median was 74. The median for the combined group was 86. The chi-square median test ($\chi^2 = 4.64$) was statistically significant (p < .05), indicating that the Head Start group was superior in verbal fluency to the non-Head Start group.

Table 3
Verbal Fluency

	Number of Children Using Indicated Number of Words	
Number of Words Used	Head Start (35)	Non-Head Start (35)
241–270	1	
211–240		2
181–210		1
151–180	5	
121–150	3	4
91–120	10	6
61–90	10	8
31–60	5	8
0–30	1	6
	Median = 96	Median = 74

Table 4
Verbal Usage

	Number of Children Giving Indicated Percentage	
Percentage of Adjectives and Adverbs	Head Start (35)	Non-Head Start (35)
24–26%	1	
21–23		
18–20		1
15–17		
12–14	3	4
9–11	10	7
6–8	8	1
3–5	8	11
0–2	5	11
	Median = 7.7%	Median = 4.8%

The distribution of scores received by subjects in verbal usage is shown in Table 4 and is expressed as the percentage of total words which were adjectives and adverbs. The percentages ranged from 0% through 26%. The median was 7.7% for the Head Start group as compared with 4.8% for the non-Head Start group. The obtained chi-square value (4.64) was statistically significant (p < .05), indicating that the Head Start group used more adjectives and adverbs in their speech.

To evaluate the child's enunciation, a rating of 1 or 2 was assigned according to the clarity of speech of the subjects on the "Describe This Picture" test. Table 5 gives the distributions of ratings for the two groups. The chi-square value obtained from the enunciation ratings ($\chi^2 = 2.81$) was not statistically significant (.05 < p > .10).

ferences between two groups on enunciation scores as large as those actually found could be expected to occur 5 to 10 percent of the time, even if chance alone were operating (i.e., program had no effect). This probability was not small enough for the investigator to reject with confidence the hypothesis that for a population of children similar to these 70, no differences on this variable would be found.

The chi-square values for verbal story-telling ability, ability to structure sentences, verbal fluency, and verbal usage were all statistically significant at less than the .05 level. The chi-square value for the enunciation rating was not statistically significant. The hypothesis that kindergarten students who participated in Project Head Start are superior in specific verbal abilities was supported except for enunciation ability.

Visual Discrimination and Naming Abilities

It was hypothesized that kindergarten children who participated in

CRITICS' NOTE:

The parenthetical expression given directly above should have been written: (.05 < p < .10). The symbol, <, means "less than." Thus, the probability of dif-

Table 5
Enunciation Ratings

Clarity of Speech Rating	Number of Children Receiving Rating	
	Head Start (35)	Non-Head Start (35)
2	22	15
1	13	20

Table 6
Naming Colors

Number of Colors Named Correctly	Number of Children with Indicated Score	
	Head Start (35)	Non-Head Start (35)
4	20	8
3	2	4
2	5	7
1	7	10
0	1	6
Median = 4.0		Median = 2.2

Project Head Start would be superior to non-Head Start children in naming colors and in naming shapes.

Table 6 presents the data obtained on the naming colors test. The range of possible colors which could be correctly identified was from 0 through 4, with one point given for each color named correctly. The median for the Head Start group was 4.0, compared to 2.2 for the non-Head Start group. The chi-square median test ($\chi^2 = 5.72$) was statistically significant (p < .025), indicating that the Head Start group was superior in the visual discrimination ability of naming colors.

Table 7 presents data showing subjects' ability to name shapes. The possible range of scores for shapes named correctly was from 0 through 3 including half points for objects named that are similar to the shapes. A medi-

an of 2.1 was obtained by the Head Start group and a median of 1.4 by the non-Head Start group. The chi-square median test ($\chi^2 = 5.72$) was statistically significant (p < .025), indicating that Head Start children were superior in naming shapes.

The chi-square values obtained for naming colors and naming shapes were statistically significant. The hypothesis that kindergarten students who participated in Project Head Start are superior in visual discrimination as measured by the ability to name correctly colors and shapes was supported by the data.

Motor Coordination Skills

The third hypothesis was that kindergarten children who participated

Table 7
Naming Shapes

Number of Shapes Named Correctly	Number of Children with Indicated Score	
	Head Start (35)	Non-Head Start (35)
3.0	9	3
2.5		
2.0	11	9
1.5	3	1
1.0	10	13
0.5		
0	2	9
	Median = 2.1	Median = 1.4

Table 8
Drawing Skill

Score on Figure Drawing Task	Number of Children with Indicated Score	
	Head Start (35)	Non-Head Start (35)
50–59	1	
40–49		
30–39	8	2
20–29	12	10
10–19	11	14
0–9	3	9
	Median = 23	Median = 16

in Project Head Start would be superior to non-Head Start children in the specific motor coordination skills of drawing, coloring, cutting, and buttoning one's clothing.

The results of the drawing task are presented in Table 8. The elements which appeared in the children's drawings were rated according to a scale set up by Goodenough (Kennedy and Lindner, 1964). The scores ranged from 0 through 59. A median of 23 was obtained for the Head Start group, compared to a median of 16 for the non-Head Start group. The chi-square median test ($\chi^2 = 4.64$) was statistically significant (p < .05). The Head Start group was thus superior in their drawing ability.

Table 9 presents the results of the coloring task. The scores had a possible range from 1 (poor) through 5 (excellent). The median was 4.8 for the Head Start group and 2.1 for the non-Head Start group. The chi-square median test

($\chi^2 = 8.28$) was statistically significant (p < .005). The Head Start group thus showed superior skill on this coloring task.

Table 10 presents the data on the cutting task. The possible range of scores was from 1 (poor) through 5 (excellent). The Head Start median was 4.7 and the non-Head Start median was 3.4. A chi-square median test was performed and the obtained value of 3.66 is slightly less than the value of 3.84 needed for significance at the .05 level. Thus, the hypothesis that the Head Start group is superior to the non-Head Start group in cutting skill could not be supported.

The results of observing buttoning skill are shown in Table 11. The subjects were given a rating of 1 if they could button their clothing by themselves and 0 if they could not. The chi-square test ($\chi^2 = 14.94$) was statistically significant (p < .001). The Head Start group thus showed superior motor co-

Table 9
Coloring Skill

	Number of Children with Indicated Score	
Score on Coloring Task	Head Start (35)	Non-Head Start (35)
5	16	8
4	6	2
3	3	3
2	2	5
1	8	17
	Median = 4.8	Median = 2.1

Table 10
Cutting Skill

	Number of Children with Indicated Score	
Score on Cutting Task	Head Start (35)	Non-Head Start (35)
5	16	8
4	5	5
3	5	8
2	4	7
1	5	7
	Median = 4.7	Median = 3.4

Table 11
Buttoning Skill

Rating	Number of Children with Indicated Score	
	Head Start (35)	Non-Head Start (35)
1	28	12
0	7	23

ordination skill in the ability to button their clothing by themselves.

The chi-square values for motor coordination skill tests of drawing, coloring, and buttoning of clothing were statistically significant at less than the .05 level. Only cutting skill resulted in a chi-square which was not statistically significant although the results were in the predicted direction. The hypothesis that kindergarten children who participated in Project Head Start are superior in certain motor coordination skills was thus generally supported by the results.

DISCUSSION

It was predicted that kindergarten children who had participated in Project Head Start would be superior to children who had no preschool experience in specific verbal abilities, visual discrimination and naming abilities, and motor coordination skills. The rationale behind this prediction was that the stated goals of the Head Start program indicated the development of these skills and abilities.

The results of this study indicate that kindergarten children who had attended the Head Start program were superior to those who had not in each of the skills and abilities tested. These results agree with the views of others who consider the preschool participation an enriching and valuable experience for the culturally deprived child.

The major speech pattern of the lower classes (Bernstein, 1960) is characterized by grammatically simple and often unfinished sentences, poor syntacti-

cal form, simple and repetitive use of conjunctions, and a rigid, limited use of adjectives and adverbs. The findings of this study regarding verbal abilities indicate that children participating in the Head Start program showed greater story-telling ability, especially in telling creative, organized stories than non-participants. They were also superior in the type of sentences employed, including the use of complex sentences. In addition the Head Start participants possessed greater verbal fluency and used a greater percentage of adjectives and adverbs. They did not, however, show greater clarity in their speech than the non-Head Start group. It appears though, that the Head Start children gained in their ability to communicate verbally. Bernstein (1960) also stated that the discriminative selection of adjectives and adverbs and the use of accurate grammatical order and complex sentence structure give direction to the organization of thinking. It is therefore likely that since the Head Start children were found to be more adept verbally, they may also be more capable of handling standard intellectual and linguistic tasks.

The results showed that the subjects in the Head Start program performed better on three of the four tests for motor coordination skill. The Head Start children were superior in drawing the figure of a man. According to Goodenough, Anastasi and D'Angelo (1952), and Anastasi and DeJesus (1953), the ability to draw a man is related to intelligence. The data indicated that the Head Start children were also superior in coloring and buttoning their clothing. Although the Head Start children also tended to do better in cutting skills, the results did not reach statistical significance.

The Head Start group was superior in visual discrimination and naming of colors and shapes. The development of these discrimination abilities is related to learning how to read which, in turn, is the basic skill needed for a successful educational experience.

In a paper by John (1963), reporting on work done at the Institute for Developmental Studies in New York, it was suggested that the middle-class child has an advantage over the lower-class child because of the tutoring available to him in his home. She emphasized that without such help it is very difficult for a child to acquire the more abstract and precise use of language. The Head Start enrichment experience may serve as a supplement to or a substitute for the home and help to develop the necessary skills and abilities early in the life of the child.

It may be that an effective enrichment program, introduced at the earliest possible time in the child's life, would prevent the cumulative deficit cited by Bernstein (1960) and Deutsch (1965b). As the child develops, it becomes progressively more difficult to reverse this deficit which increases through the years. Although some of the cumulative deficiency is associated with inadequate early preparation due to environmental deficiencies, the inadequacy of the school environment is also suggested by the researcher as a contributing cause.

The deficiencies which the home environment, inadequate educational facilities and other factors have helped to create for the culturally deprived child cannot be expected to be modified or eliminated during a summer or even in a year's enrichment program. The child's deprivation may be too deeply ingrained to be overcome in preschool and therefore this type of program should be continued throughout the early elementary grades to provide a continuity of enrichment experiences for these children. Otherwise, the results which are achieved in the preschool experience may disappear through the years as a result of crowded classrooms, inappropriate curriculum (Riessman, 1962), and other educational handicaps.

Future research should concern itself with continued examination of the values of the preschool program. These studies should be longitudinal and examine students prior, during, and for a number of years after participation in the program in order to assess the long-range benefits of the preschool program. It is vital to the success of the preschool program that the learning experiences needed to overcome the effects of the environmental limitations on children from deprived backgrounds are identified. More experimentation and exploration in this area of curriculum development for the culturally deprived child is necessary.

The experiences provided in the instructional program made it possible for children in the preschool Head Start project to become more adept in certain verbal abilities, visual discrimination abilities, and motor coordination skills. Longitudinal studies would be valuable in determining whether Head Start participants will be better school achievers than their non-Head Start counterparts as they progress in school.

SUMMARY

The purpose of this study was to assess whether the children who participated in Project Head Start were better prepared for kindergarten than those who did not participate in regard to verbal communication, visual discrimination and naming, and motor coordination skills. It was hypothesized that kindergarten children who participated in Project Head Start would be superior in verbal communication abilities as measured by verbal fluency, verbal usage, enunciation, ability to structure sentences, and ability to tell a story; that they would be superior in the visual discrimination and naming of colors and shapes; and that they would be superior in motor coordination skill, as measured by drawing figures, coloring, cutting, and buttoning their clothing.

The subjects were seventy kindergarten children between the ages of four and five who were identified on the basis of whether or not they had participated in the Head Start program during the summer of 1965. Thirty-five children who had participated in this project were paired with thirty-five children who had not participated in the project using sex, age, ethnic background, language spoken in the home, age of siblings, and preschool experience as the criteria.

The subjects were then compared with respect to their verbal communication abilities. They were asked to tell everything they saw in a sample picture and to tell a story about that picture. They were rated according to the ability to structure sentences, story-telling ability, verbal fluency, verbal usage, and enunciation.

The subjects in each group were also compared in their visual discrimination abilities. Four colors and three shapes were presented to each child who was then asked to name each color and shape. The children's productions provided data to evaluate their cutting, coloring, and drawing skills. The children's ability to button their own clothing was also observed.

The data were analyzed in terms of a comparison between the Head Start and non-Head Start groups, utilizing chi-square median tests of significance. The Head Start group did significantly better than the non-Head Start group in all hypothesized abilities and skills except for enunciation ability and cutting skill which did not reach statistical significance.

The present findings support the current view that culturally deprived children benefit from preschool enrichment programs. It was suggested that future research should further examine the values of preschool compensatory programs and establish an appropriate curriculum. Longitudinal studies are needed in order to ascertain the long-term benefits of such a program.

BIBLIOGRAPHY

ANASTASI, ANNE, & D'ANGOLO, RITA R. "A Comparison of Negro and White Children in Language Development and Goodenough Draw-A-Man IQ," *Journal of Genetic Psychology*, 1952, 81, 147–165.

ANASTASI, ANNE, & DE JESUS, GRUZ. "Language Development and Nonverbal IQ of Puerto Rican Preschool Children in New York City," *Journal of Abnormal Social Psychology*, 1953, 48, 357–366.

BERNSTEIN, B. "Language and Social Class," *British Journal of Social Class*, 1960, 271–276.

BERNSTEIN, B. "Social Class Linguistic Codes and Grammatical Elements," *Language and Speech*, 1962, 5, 221–240.

BRAIN, G. B. "An Early School Admissions Progress Report, 1963–1964," Baltimore Public Schools, September 1, 1965.

BRUNNER, CATHERINE. "Project Help: Early School Admissions Project," *Education Digest*, 1964, 29, 22–25.

BRANDT, R. M., & KYLE, D. G. "The Effect of the Early Admissions Project on Selected Cognitive Factors." Progress Report of the Baltimore Public Schools, September 1, 1965.

BUDER, L. "Head Start Gets A's for Summer," *New York Times*, October 24, 1965, 70.

DEUTSCH, CYNTHIA P. "Auditory Discrimination and Learning Social Factors," *Merrill-Palmer Quarterly of Behavior and Development*, 1964, X, 217–295.

DEUTSCH, M. "The Disadvantaged Child and the Learning Process: Some Social, Psychological and Developmental Considerations." A paper prepared by Ford Foundation Work Conference in Curriculum & Teaching in Depressed Urban Areas. New York: Columbia University Press, 1962.

DEUTSCH, M. "Early School Environment: Its Influence on School Adaptation." In D. Schreiber (Ed.), *The School Dropouts*. Washington ,D.C.: National Education Association, 1964. Pp. 89–101. (a)

DEUTSCH, M. "Facilitating Development in the Preschool Child: Social and Psychological Perspectives," *Merill-Palmer Quarterly of Behavior and Development,* 1964, X, 249–263. (b)

DEUTSCH, M. "What We've Learned About Disadvantaged Children," *Nations Schools,* 1965, 75, 50–51. (a)

DEUTSCH, M. "The Role of Social Class in Language Development and Cognition," *American Journal of Orthopsychiatry,* 1965, XXXV, 78–88 (b)

DEUTSCH, M., & BROWN, B. "Social Influences in Negro-White Intelligence Differences," *Journal of Social Issues,* 1964, 20, 24–35.

EMERY, HELEN T. "Panel of Parents Given its Okay to Head Start Plan," *New York World Telegram and Sun,* October 14, 1965, 33.

"Fast Start for Head Start," *Time Magazine,* July 2, 1965, 64.

FOWLER, W. "Cognitive Learning in Infancy and Early Childhood," *Psychological Bulletin,* 1962, No. 59, 116–152.

GRAHAM, J., & HESS, R. *Handbook for Project Head Start.* Chicago: University of Chicago Press, 1965.

HECHINGER, F. M. "Head Start Falls Behind," *New York Times,* December 5, 1965, E9. (a)

HECHINGER, F. M. "Head Start to Where," *Saturday Review,* December

18, 1965, 58–60, 75. (b)

HENRY, J. *Culture Against Man.* New York: Random House, 1963.

HESS, R. D., & ROSEN, A. *Condensed Inventory of Preschool Projects.* Chicago: University of Chicago Press, 1965.

"Hopeful Head Start," *Time Magazine,* September 10, 1965, 17.

HUNT, J. M. "The Psychological Basis for Using Preschool Enrichment as an Antidote for Cultural Deprivation," *Merill-Palmer Quarterly of Behavior and Development,* 1964, X, 209–248.

Institute for Developmental Studies. *Annual Report 1965.* New York: New York Medical College, 1965.

JENSEN, A. "Learning in the Preschool Years," *Journal of Nursery Education,* 1963, 18, 133–138.

JOHN, VERA P. "The Intellectual Development of Slum Children: Some Preliminary Findings," *American Journal of Orthopsychiatry,* 1963, 33, 813–822.

JOHN, VERA P., & GOLDSTEIN, L. S. "The Social Context of Language Acquisition," *Merill-Palmer Quarterly of Behavior and Development,* 1964, 10, 265–275.

KENDLER, T. S. "Development of Mediating Responses in Children," *Monographs of the Society for Research in Child Development,* 1963, 28, No. 86, 33–48.

KENNEDY, W. A., & LINDNER, R. S. "A Normative Study of the Goodenough Draw-A-Man Test on Southeastern Negro Elementary School Children," *Child Development,* 1964, 35, 33–61.

KLINEBERG, O. "Negro-White Differences in Intelligence Test Performance: A New Look at an Old Problem," *American Psychologist,* 1963, 8, 198–203.

KURZ, H. "Schools Pass Up Class Expansion under Head Start," *New York World Telegram and Sun,* November 30, 1965, 31.

"Let's Make Head Start Regular Start," *Ebony Magazine*, September, 1965, 96.

MONTAGUE, D. O. "Arithmetic Concepts of Kindergarten Children in Contrasting Socio-economic Areas," *Elementary School Journal*, 1964, 64, 393–397.

NEWTON, M. R. "Crisis Intervention in Preschool and Early School Years: The Sumter Child Study Project." Paper read at 42nd annual American Orthopsychiatric Association Meeting, March, 1965.

PHILLIPS, ADELAIDE. "Pre-kindergarten Program: New Haven, Connecticut, 1963-Ongoing." Progress report of the New Haven Public School System, 1965.

"Preschool Programs Strive to Start Deprived Children on Par with Others," *Nations Schools*, June 1964, 84.

RIESSMAN, F. *The Culturally Deprived Child*. New York: Harper and Row, 1962.

RIVERA, C. "Oral English Program for Non-English-speaking Children, El Paso, Texas." Progress Report of the El Paso Public School System, November 2, 1965.

STEELE, J. "Head Start Bogged Down by Red Tape," *New York World Telegram and Sun*, December 1, 1965, 12.

STINE, O., & SARATISIOTIS, J. "Evaluation of Project Help's Instructional Program on the Physical and Emotional Health of the Project Pupil." Progress report of the Baltimore Public Schools, September 1, 1965.

CRITIQUE

1. QUESTION:

According to the investigator, "The purpose of this study was to evaluate whether the children who participated in Project Head Start were better prepared for kindergarten than those who did not participate. . . ." To accomplish this purpose, the investigator: 1) reviewed the literature, 2) stated hypotheses, 3) selected subjects, 4) selected and constructed measuring instruments, 5) administered and scored tests, 6) performed data analyses, and 7) drew conclusions.

A.   What two importantly different kinds of information are contained in the review of the literature? What, in general, are the main purposes of any review of the literature and how well did the investigator succeed in achieving these purposes?

B.   Write a critical appraisal of each of the other six aspects of the study identified above. That is, write one or more paragraphs about each of the following: how the hypotheses were stated, how the subjects were selected, how the measuring instruments were selected and constructed, etc. Be sure to cite strengths as well as weaknesses.

1A.   ANSWER:

One kind of information in Kaplan's literature review is the description of the social and political forces which in 1965 were changing drastically the prekindergarten public education of economically and socially disadvantaged children. The Kaplan report indicates that by 1965 Project Head Start "benefited" 560,000 youngsters in 2,500 communities at an estimated cost of $112,000,000. A second kind of information in the literature review is more commonly found. The investigator cites empirical studies (e.g., Bernstein, 1960, 1962; Deutsch, 1956b) and studies of new educational practices (Graham and Hess, 1965; Hess and Rosen, 1965).

One main purpose of a review of literature section in empirical studies is to describe the educational context in sufficient detail such that the justification of the study is clear. The literature review succeeds fairly well in giving us the political, historical, and empirical context of the study. These political and social changes in educational practice which the investigator documents serve as an excellent stimulus and justification for educational research.[1]

A second main purpose of a review is to indicate the *source* of con-

---

[1] Among social scientists and educational researchers there often exists a tension between being socially relevant ("on a white horse") and scientifically rigorous ("wearing a white coat"). Whenever social changes take place rapidly and pervasively, the tension can develop into a rift. In our opinion this division is unnecessary and counterproductive. Social changes can be thought of as an excellent stimulus to empirical inquiry, as we indicate about the Kaplan study. More than that, the empirical researcher who can say as a result of inquiry that he knows both the fact and the educational consequences of political and policy decisions can become a valuable influence upon the shaping of future educational policies. Many researchers would prefer to spend money on research *before* changes are made so that they might be made intelligently in the light of new knowledge. Social urgencies dictate otherwise sometimes. Perhaps the best course is to combine the two: research can change policy and practice, and changes in policy and practice can be valuable stimuli to further research. For a discussion of some of these issues, see Nevitt Sanford, *The American College* (New York: John Wiley, 1962), pp. 1–30.

cepts and principles used to *guide* the inquiry. One can find instances in which the evaluation was influenced by the empirical studies and writing quoted in the review. One example of the influence of these sources on the conduct of the inquiry is the literature which points to the need for emphasis on language teaching for the disadvantaged. This information justifies the inclusion of language development measures in the study.

A third main purpose is to provide a theoretical context from which the knowledge claims of the inquiry can receive intelligible interpretation. There is none of this material in the review. Some readers would say that the large differences found after a short summer program are rather remarkable, yet there is no theoretical context, nor even an educational rationale, provided which can help us to account for or make sense out of these findings.

1B.   ANSWER:

1.   Hypotheses

2.   Subjects

3.   Measuring Instruments (selection and construction)

4.　Test Administration and Scoring

5.　Analysis

6.　Investigator's Conclusions

1.　Hypotheses

The "Hypotheses" (see p. 28) presents a clear statement of the questions to which the investigator is seeking answers. Although it is not always necessary for questions to be in the form of hypotheses in which predicted results are stated, we approve of the investigator's indication in this section of the direction in which she predicts the results will appear. Most experts favor directionally stated scientific hypotheses to those expressed in the less communicative null form.

In assessing the hypotheses, several student readers questioned the investigator's methods of measurement, the failure to consider other variables in the study, and the feasibility of matching students. Valid as these concerns may be, for convenience they will not be considered at this point in our assessment of the study.

2. *Subjects*

The principal technical flaw in the evaluation is that no control was exercised over the assignment of children to Head Start or control programs. Further, because such variables as sex, ethnic background, age (only a 10-month range), language spoken in the home, and age of siblings would not be expected to be *highly* correlated with the measures used in the study, the reader has little assurance that the two groups being compared were initially equal in those skills and abilities the Head Start program most wanted to affect. The investigator also mentioned this problem (see p. 30).

We could assess more accurately the likelihood of this initial equality if we were told in the report the reasons why the control children did not attend Head Start classes. Did they live too far away from the Head Start center, come from more stable homes, or live in better neighborhoods? Did the control children not attend Head Start programs because their parents chose not to send them? If so, then differences in attitudes toward education (as seen by differences in the learning experiences provided in the home—learning experiences such as talking, reading, color identification, etc.) could mean that the Head Start children would have scored higher than the control children even before the Head Start experience was begun, and certainly after an additional year of a better learning situation in the home.

The investigator was wise not to match students on intelligence or other cognitive or attitude variables measured *after* the Head Start experience. If the Head Start program improved the children's scores on such variables, then matching children on their scores would cancel the very effects to be demonstrated.

Suppose the investigator had been able to administer identical criterion measures (verbal fluency, enunciation, etc.) *before* the Head Start experience and to match children on the basis of their scores on such measures. Differences between the two groups would still be expected on these measures when the children were tested in kindergarten, *even if the Head Start program had no effect* in developing the skills and abilities measured by the criterion tests. Such bogus or false differences can be explained by the regression phenomenon.[2]

We do not fault the investigator for matching students. We merely wish to point out that such matching was probably largely ineffective in assuring the equality of the two groups prior to training. Matching on variables measured *before* the Head Start programs were begun *and* which were more highly related to the criterion variables would have been far preferable. But even if this were done, the lack of random assignment of children to the Head Start and control conditions still prevents the ruling out of selection bias and regression artifacts.

---

[2] For an elementary discussion of the regression phenomenon, read: Kenneth D. Hopkins, "Regression and the Matching Fallacy in Quasi-Experimental Research," *Journal of Special Education,* 1969, 3, 329–336.

Frequently expressed reactions of student readers are that 35 children per group is too small a number and the number of Head Start programs being evaluated is not mentioned in the article. More data are always desirable, but an investigator must weigh the increased scope against the increased "costs" associated with having a larger sample size. The differences between the Head Start and control groups were sufficiently great that 35 cases per group were adequate to reject for most of the variables the "chance alone" null hypothesis. Perhaps more useful than a larger sample size would be having as a sample children taken from several Head Start programs. We suspect, but are not certain, that all the children were exposed to the same program and, if this was the case, the generalizability of the results is very uncertain.

3. Measuring Instruments (selection and construction)

Given the rather limited goal of assessing the comparative performances of the two groups of children, then ideally the measuring instruments used in the study should represent a diverse collection of reliable and valid devices for measuring the degree to which the intended skills and abilities have been developed and undesirable unintended ones are absent.

Many student readers objected to the absence of test reliability and validity data in the report. If a test is unreliable, then it is not measuring any trait or skill consistently; the test score then has a large component of random error. Such inconsistency of measurement and random error are to be avoided since real treatment effects are obscured by such unreliable instruments. In the context of this study, Head Start programs cannot be judged effective if the measures of effectiveness are largely unreliable. Since the investigator did find group differences, we can assume that the instruments employed had at least sufficient reliability to demonstrate what was desired.

"Narrowly considered, *validation* is the process of examining the accuracy of a specific prediction or inference made from a test score. . . . One validates, not a test, but an *interpretation of data arising from a specific procedure.*"[3] The investigator would probably claim that the test items are representative instances of the skills being described and, thus, her inferences about children's capabilities based on their test performance are valid. Such a claim seems reasonable to us with possibly two exceptions. First, we question whether the Goodenough Draw-a-Man-Test is as much a measure of motor coordination as it is an indicator of other skills. Second, we have some slight qualms about the buttoning-own-clothes measure since the task is not the same for all children. (Some children had clothes harder to button than others.)

Because the specific Head Start programs being evaluated were not described, we do not know for sure the extent to which the abilities and

---

[3] Lee J. Cronbach, "Test Validation," Chapter 14 in Robert L. Thorndike (Ed.), *Educational Measurement* (Washington, D.C.: American Council on Education, 1971).

skills measured by the tests used in this study represent the primary objectives of these programs. Further, we do not know the extent to which the very tasks used in the tests were used in the training programs themselves. This is not to say that it would be wrong to use identical tasks in both teaching and testing. It is just that interpretation of group differences and the value of a program depend upon knowing the relation of tasks tested to the tasks used in training.

We suggest that in an evaluation study of this type three categories of tasks be used in the testing: (1) those tasks directly involved in the training (on which large group differences favoring the Head Start group would be expected); (2) tasks not used in the training but on which it is hoped there will be group differences; and (3) tasks representing unintended outcomes (on which there are no particular expectations).

We wished more of the category two and category three tasks were used in this evaluation. As examples of category two tasks, we would like to have seen the differences in performance of the two groups on tasks requiring left-right visual search and production of graphic symbols (e.g., letters). In addition, as a category two or three task, measures of personal-social adjustment to school would have also been of interest.

The investigator is to be commended, however, for including several measures of performance rather than relying on just one or two. Where there were no standardized tests to measure the type of performance on which the investigator wished to compare the groups, she devised her own tests for these skills and abilities. This, too, is commendable.

4. Test Administration and Scoring

The importance of administering tests prior to the start of the Head Start program was mentioned earlier.

The investigator indicated that the instruments were administered, ". . . at the beginning of kindergarten in order to insure that these skills and abilities to be tested were not learned during the kindergarten experience [p. 30]. Although there is some merit to this procedure, we feel it would have been desirable if some of the tests had also been administered at the end of kindergarten, or even later. The critical importance of ascertaining the *long-term* benefits of Head Start programs has been well documented by the investigator herself. The advantage of the Head Start group during the first weeks of the school year may be due primarily to preschool environment and materials which have no carry-over effect on later learning. Although determining if there is an immediate effect is useful, it would be of great value to document that a primary goal of Head Start programs, increased performance in school, was met.

Recall that the measuring was not blinded from the standpoint of the observer, although the investigator claims on page 30 to have made no effort to remember which children were in the Head Start group. This is small comfort to the reader who suspects that the children's membership in either group could have been independently identified and thus could have biased the judgment of the investigator as she administered and scored the tests.

The testing was somewhat subjective, both in administration (e.g., frequency of directions to be given, probing for termination of responses) and scoring. (See especially the cutting, coloring, and enunciation tests.) Thus, the results were open to the influence of the evaluator herself. The investigator is not to be faulted for using instruments which were subjective in nature. However, using these instruments in such a manner that the subjective element invalidates the comparison between the two groups is a procedure open to criticism.

5. Analysis

The analysis of the data was adequate and not misleading even though more precise statistical techniques could have been employed. The investigator could have utilized the exact scores and not have forced them into two categories (above and below the combined median). Further, the investigator could have made use of the fact that she had matched pairs of children. However, these objections carry little weight since the result of substituting these more refined techniques would have been more power (i.e., likelihood of rejecting false "no difference" hypotheses) and almost all of the chance-alone or no difference hypotheses were rejected even without their use.

The investigator is to be commended for not evidencing an unthinking attachment to a particular criterion of statistical significance. (See the Critics' Notes on page 31 for an explanation of the 5 percent criterion used by the investigator.) Particularly in the case of the cutting-skill variable, the evaluator showed her willingness to accept evidence of a difference even though the obtained test statistic fell somewhat short of the critical value needed to claim statistical significance at the 5 percent level.

6. Investigator's Conclusions

The investigator is quite correct in stating that, ". . . kindergarten children who had attended the Head Start program were superior to those who had not in each of the skills and abilities tested." This conclusion is merely a factual statement of the results found. Even though a few differences did not reach statistical significance, it is a fact that the Head Start group had superior scores on all the measures.

The investigator is also permitted to say, "The findings support the current view that culturally deprived children benefit from preschool programs [p. 38]." "Findings support the current view" is interpreted to mean that the findings are consistent with the current view, and it does *not* imply that the results prove that the children benefited from the programs.

Because of the lack of fundamental controls as specified earlier in our appraisal, we have no assurance that the differences were due to the Head Start programs. Thus, we feel the investigator is not justified in making conclusions that imply the Head Start programs caused the superior performance. We question the validity of such a conclusion as: "The experiences provided in the instructional program made it possible for children in the preschool Head Start project to become more adept. . . . [p. 37]."

Finally, before claiming that results will generalize to other Head Start projects, we would want to see such positive results from a larger sample of students and programs.

2. QUESTION:

The investigator evidently feels that the Head Start programs involved in her study were very effective and worthwhile. Yet there is information needed in addition to that given in the report if one is to reproduce such an effective program elsewhere. What information is lacking in the report which prevents it from serving as a guide to one who must develop and operate a Head Start program? (Assume that the leader has much freedom in how he plans and runs a Head Start program.)

2. ANSWER:

To develop and operate a Head Start program effectively, one would need to have much financial, legal, and political information not touched upon in the report. To plan the instructional aspects of the program, that is, to decide what to teach and how and when to teach it, a detailed specification of the Head Start programs being evaluated in the present article is needed. Lack of this specification is a major deficiency of this report.

The reader is left completely in the dark as to the components of the programs, their duration, the training and number of staff, the objectives of the programs, the procedures used to achieve these objectives, and so on. *Without even the most rudimentary description of the programs, the investigator has produced an evaluation report not unlike a research report in which the independent variable was unspecified.* As the report now stands, its nearly total neglect of description of the programs makes it of use only to a small number of persons who are intimately acquainted with the programs being evaluated. No two Head Start programs are alike. Without a description of the programs herein evaluated, we do not know what programs to perpetuate or how the programs should be conducted differently. What good is an evaluation that something works when that "something" is an enigma?

5

Prediction of Long-Term Success in Doctoral Work in Psychology[*1]

J. Richard Hackman / Nancy Wiggins
Alan R. Bass

This study examines the degree to which measures of aptitude and undergraduate preparation obtained before the beginning of doctoral study are predictive of the "success" of psychology graduate students. Criterion measures were taken at two points in time. At the end of the first year of graduate study, the general progress and potential of each student was rated, and first-year course grades were obtained. Judgments of the overall success of each student were made six years after the beginning of graduate work, when all students in the research either had completed a Ph.D. or had withdrawn from

* Originally appeared in Educational and Psychological Measurement, Summer 1970, pp. 365–374. Reprinted with permission of the publisher and senior author.
[1] The authors wish to thank the personnel of the Graduate Records Office of the Department of Psychology at the University of Illinois for their considerable help in obtaining the data on which the present report is based, and Douglas T. Hall, Benjamin Schneider, and David Hamilton for their comments on a draft of this paper.

doctoral study. Thus, the study provides a relatively unusual opportunity to examine the degree to which long-term success in psychology doctoral work can be predicted from pre-enrollment data. In addition, it is possible to determine the degree to which evaluations made at the end of the first year of doctoral work are congruent with the long-term assessments of success in the program.

METHOD—Subjects

Subjects were 42 students who began doctoral work in psychology at the University of Illinois in 1963. The sample includes the entire class of students entering the doctoral program that year except for a small number of individuals who had completed some graduate work elsewhere.

Predictors

Four groups of predictors were obtained from the application materials submitted by the students to the University.

Aptitude and Ability Measures

Three scales from the Graduate Record Examination were used: (a) verbal aptitude (GRE-V); (b) quantitative aptitude (GRE-Q); and (c) the advanced test in psychology (GRE-A).

Indicators of Foreign Language Facility

At the time of the study, reading ability in two foreign languages was required for the doctorate at the University of Illinois, and three indicators of the foreign language competence of the students were collected: (a) the number of languages students indicated that they spoke; (b) the number of languages students indicated that they read; and (c) the number of semester hours of language taken as an undergraduate.

Undergraduate Academic Performance

Data relevant to the overall academic performance of the students, and of their performance in particular fields potentially useful for graduate study in psychology were compiled. In particular, undergraduate grade-point averages were obtained for: (a) all courses in the junior and senior years (GPA-overall); (b) all psychology courses (GPA-psych); (c) all mathematics courses (GPA-math); (d) all physical science courses except for biology (GPA-science); (e) all biology courses (GPA-biology); and (f) all sociology courses (GPA-soc). Data from student transcripts were converted, when necessary, to a 5-point grade scale (fail = 1.0).

Quality of Undergraduate Institution

Overall ratings of the academic quality of the undergraduate college or university from which the student came were made by a committee of the University of Illinois psychology department faculty members. A 3-point scale was used: (1) the school is of dubious academic quality; (2) the school is of average academic quality; and (3) the school is of excellent academic quality. Judgments were made by consensus, and reliability data are not available.

CRITERIA—First-Year Criteria

Data collected at the end of the first year of doctoral study included grades in graduate courses, each student's personal assessment of his progress and prognosis, and the judgments of faculty members of progress toward the degree.

Measures of classroom performance obtained were: (a) grades in the first and second semesters of Proseminar in Psychology—a broad and intensive coverage of all major content fields in psychology; (b) grades in the first and second semesters of Quantitative Methods—an intensive coverage of most major topics in experimental design and statistical analysis; and (c) the end-of-year grade point average, which included grades in the two "core" courses as well as grades in other elective courses.

Students reported perceptions of their progress toward the Ph.D. on a 5-point scale, ranging from "very rapidly" to "very slowly" at the end of the first year. In addition, students indicated whether or not they planned to continue their graduate studies in psychology at the University of Illinois.

Two faculty assessments of student performance at the end of the year were obtained. Faculty members rated all first-year students whom they had had in a course as to whether the student should be encouraged to continue for the Ph.D. The 4-point scale ranged from "encourage to go ahead for the Ph.D." to "advise to drop out of graduate school immediately." An average was taken for each student of all ratings made of him by departmental faculty members. In addition, an overall assessment was made at the end of the year by the head of each departmental division (experimental, clinical, social-measurement). This assessment was coded onto a 6-point scale, ranging from "excellent progress, assured of financial aid" to "dropped from graduate program, no degree possible."

Long-Term Criterion

Six years after the students began their graduate work, all of them had either obtained a Ph.D. or had withdrawn from the program. At the time each student left the University (either with or without the Ph.D.), notation was made of where he was going and the circumstances of his leaving. Interviews were held with a sample of departmental faculty members regarding what constitutes "success" for a psychology doctoral student. On the basis of these interviews, a 9-point scale was constructed to reflect how successful, in the eyes of departmental faculty, each of the students in the sample was. The scale ranged from: "obtained the Ph.D. and accepted an academic or professional appointment at a highly prestigious institution" to "was dropped from the doctoral program on academic grounds in the first year of graduate study." Two judges placed each of the 42 students on the 9-point scale, and the inter-judge reliability was .95.

RESULTS

Relationships between the predictors and both end-of-first-year and long-term criteria are presented in Table 1. There is a very strong relationship between the quality of a student's undergraduate institution and his overall success in the doctoral program as assessed six years after he began graduate study. The quality of the undergraduate school also is significantly related to the student's own perceptions of his progress toward the degree after one year of study, and to faculty ratings of his progress at that time.

Graduate Record Examination verbal and quantitative scores are positively related to many of the first year criteria, but only GRE-Q is significantly related to the long-term criterion. GRE-Q does not relate to performance in the core content courses the first year, which might be expected, since the core content courses do not demand quantitative skills or sophistication. The GRE advanced test in psychology does not relate significantly to any of the criteria except for the first semester core content course.

Although undergraduate grade-point average in psychology does relate positively to grades in some first year graduate courses, other GPA measures tend to relate *negatively* to all other criteria, especially the long-term criterion of success. All six of the GPA measures are negatively correlated with the long-term criterion, two of them significantly so.

Also negatively related to the long-term criterion (and to a number of the first-year criteria) are the three measures of foreign language facility.

Relationships between the first-year and long-term criteria are presented in Table 2. Grades in the first year courses do not, in general, relate significantly to the long-term criterion of success. It is clear, however, that by the end of the first year both the student and the faculty have a fairly good estimation of the student's progress and his potential for the doctorate. Both of the student reports and both of the faculty judgments of how the student is progressing relate significantly and substantially to the long-term criterion.

DISCUSSION

The present study provides a partial replication of results reported by

Table 1
Predictor-Criterion Relationships

	End-of-first-year Criteria					Self-reports:		Faculty ratings:		Long-term Criterion
	Core Content Course I	Core Content Course II	Core Quantitative Course I	Core Quantitative Course II	End of Year GPA	Speed to Degree	Plans to Continue	Making Normal Progress	Encourage toward Ph. D.	Global Assessment of "success" six years after enrollment
Aptitude and Ability										
GRE-Verbal	.30*	.14	.26	.03	.22	.45*	.23	.21	.20	.19
GRE-Quant.	−.12	−.05	.56*	.50*	.15	.40*	.03	.29	.23	.32*
GRE-Advanced (Psych.)	.35*	.24	.13	−.14	.23	.23	.16	.08	.12	−.11
Foreign Language facility										
No. languages spoken	−.42*	.05	.19	.28	.04	−.04	−.39*	−.04	.10	−.21
No. languages read	−.29	.29	.28	.33*	.19	.07	−.47*	.01	.28	−.25
No. hours language taken as undergrad.	−.10	.07	−.03	−.13	−.06	−.20	−.25	−.03	−.02	−.34*
Undergraduate grades										
GPA last two yrs.	.24	.29	−.04	.07	.28	.02	−.04	−.08	.05	−.22
GPA psychology	.24	.31*	.04	.22	.34*	.14	.20	.21	.07	−.05
GPA mathematics	.13	.13	.06	.21	.22	.20	−.14	−.02	.22	−.28
GPA phys. science	−.12	.01	−.07	−.08	−.19	−.17	.00	−.32*	−.24	.50*
GPA biology	.06	.14	−.22	.03	.04	−.09	−.14	−.32*	−.05	.31*
GPA sociology	.11	.13	−.19	.29	.20	.12	.02	−.09	.17	−.02
Rated Quality Undergrad. School	.00	−.13	.21	.16	.15	.30*	.16	.31*	.08	.43*

$N = 42$.

* $p = < .05$.

53

Table 2
Relationships between First-year and Long-term Criteria

End-of-first-year Criteria	Global assessment of "success" six years after enrollment
Course Grades	
Core Content Course I	.28
Core Content Course II	−.08
Core Quantitative Course I	.19
Core Quantitative Course II	.28*
End-of-year GPA	.24
Self-reports	
Speed to degree	.50*
Plans to continue	.45*
Faculty ratings	
Making normal progress	.56*
Encourage toward Ph. D.	.35*

$N = 42$.
* $p < .05$ (one-tailed).

Wiggins, Blackburn, and Hackman (1969) on the relationships between pre-enrollment predictors and end-of-first-year grades. The Wiggins et al., study reported data for students entering the doctoral program in psychology at the University of Illinois in 1965 and 1966 and included a total of 104 students. It was found that GRE-V was not significantly predictive of first year grades (except for one significant relationship for a Core Content course in one sample), and that GRE-Q significantly related only to Core Quantitative course grades. GRE advanced test scores related significantly to grades in both semesters of the Core Content courses and to overall end-of-first-year GPA. These findings are generally consistent with the present results.

In addition, Wiggins et al., found that the rated quality of a student's undergraduate institution did not relate significantly to first year grades, and that overall undergraduate GPA related significantly to grades in the Core Content courses. Again, these results tend to be consistent with the direction (if not always with the level of statistical significance attained) of the results of the present study.

It should be noted, however, that the Wiggins et al., study used as criteria only *grades* earned during the *first year* of graduate work. The present study shows that the pattern of results changes substantially when one uses criteria of progress towards the Ph.D. other than grades, and especially when one examines the long-term "success" of the student. For example, the quality of the undergraduate school, which predicted first year grades negligibly, was found to be significantly related to student and faculty global assessments of progress toward the Ph.D. at the end of the year, and correlated more substantially than any other predictor with the long-term criterion of success. On the other hand, undergraduate grades and the GRE advanced test in psychology tended to correlate positively with first year grades (especially grades in the Core Content courses), but were *negatively* related to the long-term criterion.

Thus, it appears that first year grades themselves may not be good indicators of the progress and potential of psychology graduate students. Subjective assessments by students and faculty of progress toward the Ph.D. obtained at the end of the first year do, however, tend to be related to the predictors in very much the same pattern as is the long-term criterion. The implication is that both students and faculty have a fairly good idea of how the student is doing at the end of his first year and how he will ultimately turn out as a graduate student, but that data in addition to course grades are important in developing that subjective assessment. It may be that students get "labelled" either as promising or as not promising students very early in their graduate careers. These labels may tend to remain attached throughout the student's doctoral work and thereby affect the kinds of job opportunities which are available to students when they complete their degrees. To the extent that one input to the "labelling" process is the quality of the undergraduate institution from which a student comes, the strong empirical links among the quality of undergraduate school, faculty assessments at the end of the first year, and long-term rated success would not be unexpected. Indeed, it may be that in some cases the labels attached to students could lead to the creation of self-fulfilling prophesies of successful or unsuccessful work in graduate school— and desirable or undesirable job offers thereafter.

One of the most unexpected findings of the present study is the consistently negative correlations obtained between undergraduate grades in all fields of study and the long-term criterion. To further explore this finding, the correlations among the predictors were examined. These data are presented in Table 3.

The several GPA measures were correlated among themselves fairly highly, as would be expected. In addition, however, there is a consistent tendency for the GPA predictors to relate negatively to the rated quality of the undergraduate school. This raises the possibility that the reason for the negative correlations between the GPA scores and the long-term criterion is that some students earned very high grades at poor quality institutions—

and did poorly in their doctoral work, whereas other students earned only moderate grades at quite high quality (and, by implication, tougher) schools —and did well in their doctoral work. To check this possibility, partial correlations were computed between the several undergraduate GPA scores and the long-term criterion, partialling out the quality of the undergraduate school. The correlations remained consistently negative (ranging from $-.09$ to $-.45$), suggesting that all of the negative relationship found between undergraduate GPA and success as a doctoral student is not due to the differential ease of earning high grades at undergraduate schools of varying quality. The finding remains, therefore, something of an enigma, and surely deserving of further investigation.

Finally, a word should be said regarding the negative relationships between foreign language facility and the long-term criterion. At the time the data were collected, reading ability in two foreign languages was a prerequisite for the Ph.D. at the University of Illinois, and it was expected that having a "head start" toward meeting this requirement might substantially enhance the performance of students in the doctoral program. This expectation was disconfirmed and, indeed, it appears that having taken a large number of foreign language courses as an undergraduate (and thus having better than average facility in languages) may somehow be *dysfunctional* for progress toward the degree.

SUMMARY

The usefulness of measures of aptitude and undergraduate preparation in predicting long-term as well as short-term success in a psychology graduate program was examined. Subjects were 42 students who enrolled in the University of Illinois graduate program in psychology in 1963. Graduate Record Ex-

Table 3
Relationships among the Predictors

	1	2	3	4	5	6	7	8	9	10	11	12	13
1. GRE-V	—												
2. GRE-Q	.24	—											
3. GRE-A	.60*	-.02	—										
4. Number of languages spoken	-.25	.10	-.33*	—									
5. Number of languages read	-.03	.20	-.06*	.65*	—								
6. Number of undergraduate hours of language	-.05	.05	.21	-.02	.20	—							
7. GPA-overall	.04	-.22	.18	.04	-.11	.14	—						
8. GPA-Psych	.16	.18	.15	.02	-.04	.04	.75*	—					
9. GPA-Math	-.27	.00	-.07	.17	.12	.11	.52*	.35*	—				
10. GPA-Science	-.17	-.17	.08	.17	.07	.20	.27	.15	.39*	—			
11. GPA-Biology	-.16	-.19	-.14	.30*	.12	-.15	.48*	.28	.51*	.52*	—		
12. GPA-Sociology	-.26	.07	-.08	.18	.13	.22	.49*	.39*	.65*	.40*	.34*	—	
13. Quality of undergraduate school	.22	.30*	.24	.20	-.09	-.20	-.33*	-.26	-.39*	-.25	-.28	-.35*	—

$N = 42$.
* $p < .05$.

56

amination scores and undergraduate grade point average were found to significantly predict first year grades in graduate courses, but to be inconsistently and sometimes significantly negatively related to a global assessment of "success" in the doctoral program made six years after enrollment. Rated quality of the student's undergraduate school was not related to performance in first year graduate courses, but was significantly positively related to the long-term criterion. Facility in foreign languages at the time of enrollment tended to be negatively related to both short-term and long-term criteria.

REFERENCE

WIGGINS, N., BLACKBURN, MARGARET, and HACKMAN, J. R. The prediction of first year graduate success in psychology: Peer ratings. *Journal of Educational Research,* 1969, 63, 81–85.

C R I T I Q U E

1. QUESTION:

What were the investigators hoping to achieve? That is, what was the purpose(s) of the study?

1. ANSWER:

We think the investigators had two primary purposes which are well stated in the opening and closing sentences of the initial paragraph of the article: (a) to examine, ". . . the degree to which measures of aptitude and undergraduate preparation obtained before the beginning of doctoral study are predictive of the (short and long-term) 'success' of psychology graduate students."; (b) ". . . to determine the degree to which evaluations made at the end of the first year of doctoral work are congruent with the long-term assessments of success in the program." The relationships mentioned in purposes (a) and (b) above are shown in Tables 1 and 2 respectively.

STUDENT RESPONSES. Several students who read this study inferred that the investigators were trying to make predictions rather than "just to gather information" about relationships between predictors and criteria. They claim that, ". . . the purpose of the study was to find a kind of cause/ effect relationship, so that the Graduate School at the University of Illinois or other graduate schools can make specific recommendations to undergraduate institutions, to future students, and to faculty members about changing or maintaining certain practices."

OUR REPLY.   Worthwhile as the purpose of developing a prediction system might be, the investigators did not state it as their aim. If their purpose were to devise a prediction system which could be used by educators, they no doubt would have then followed the recommended practice of cross-validating their results; that is, trying out the system on a student group different from that used to develop the prediction formula.[1]

2. QUESTION:

A.   How many specific pre-enrollment predictors (not groups or categories) were used? Your answer should be a specific numerical value.

B.   How many specific criteria were used?

C.   Was it a good idea to employ so many variables in a single study? Why or why not?

2. ANSWER:

A.   Thirteen predictors were used. These predictors are listed in the left-hand column of Tables 1 and 3 as well as in the body of the article.

B.   Ten criteria were employed; all but one of these are considered short-term criteria. These criteria are listed at the tops of the columns in Table 1, in Table 2, and in the body of the article.

C.   We approve of using multiple predictors and criteria in any study for two reasons. First, we are rarely interested in a dependent variable which can be perfectly measured by a single variable. A good case in point is the present study in which "success" is clearly a complex concept—the

---

[1] For an entertaining account of how failure to cross-validate a prediction system can lead to astounding and unfounded claims, read: Edward Cureton, "Reliability, Validity and Baloney," *Educational and Psychological Measurement*, 1950, 10, 94–96.

more aspects of success we study the better. Second, the more independent, or predictor, variables included in a study, the more information we obtain about the relationships we are interested in. Study of a greater network of interrelationships aids in comprehending and explaining the reasons for the relationships.

On the other hand, use of variables poorly measured or lacking rationale for inclusion should not be encouraged. It should be kept in mind that when a great many relationships are studied, it is probable that some bogus, seemingly "significant" ones will appear. Thus, caution is required in interpreting isolated findings. Further, for statistical reasons involving the stability of the prediction equation coefficients, there are too many predictors for so few students to construct a *prediction* system that would be expected to work well (cross-validate) on a different sample. The investigators were wise to focus their analyses on simple, two-variable *relationships*.

3.   QUESTION:

The predictors used are categorized into four groups:

(a)   Aptitude and ability
(b)   Foreign language facility
(c)   Undergraduate grades
(d)   Rated quality of undergraduate school

Evaluate the appropriateness of the specific measures employed in each group of predictors. In your answer, focus upon whether these measures were reasonable choices and *not* upon whether, in fact, they seemed to work in this particular study.

3.   ANSWER:

(a)   Aptitude and Ability Predictors

(b)   Foreign Language Facility

(c)   Undergraduate Academic Performance

(d)   Quality of Undergraduate Institution

3.   ANSWER:

(a)   Aptitude and Ability Predictors

At least for short-term success, aptitude measures have been shown to be good predictors. The Graduate Record Examination (GRE) tests are widely employed and have proved useful in the past. The GRE correlations serve as a useful benchmark against which to judge the magnitude of relationships found with other predictors. Both past performance and current practice argue for inclusion of these test scores.

(b)   Foreign Language Facility

Unfortunately the reader has to wait until the very end of the paper before he is given the rationale for including these predictors. The argument is not terribly convincing. We have no objection to the inclusion of foreign language facility but suspect more interesting and meaningful predictors could have been found. The three specific measures employed in this category leave much to be desired as true indicators of foreign language facility. They may have been used because they were handy. Their inclusion is no crime; it is just that they are not apt to be very enlightening.

STUDENT RESPONSES.   In the evaluation of several of these predictors, as well as in the evaluation of some of the criteria (see Question 4 below), a large number of students were critical of the *subjectivity* involved in the measures. Many students went so far as to say that some measures were "worthless" or "should not be used" because they were subjective.

OUR REPLY.   "Subjectivity" can have two meanings. In one sense, subjectivity means based on personal experience or a matter of opinion. In another sense, it means unreliable and that judges do not agree. A doctor should not dismiss a patient's complaint of pain because it is based on personal experience or because other judges cannot agree on the amount of pain involved. Likewise, we would caution researchers against an off-hand dismissal of all subjective measurements. The phenomena we may have the greatest difficulty measuring will sometimes be those most worth measuring. One must often ask whether it is better to measure something trivial well or to measure something important less well. No simple answer is possible.

(c)   Undergraduate Academic Performance

It is wise to include these predictors for the same reasons that the aptitude measures should be included. Of course, grades from different institutions are not completely comparable since a C at one institution may show greater achievement than a B at another institution. Nevertheless, even with such a deficiency, grades have been found to be useful predictors in the past and should be included.

Analyzing the grade record by specific course has the advantage of making the grades somewhat comparable, although this comparability is achieved at the loss of reliability. Grade averages based on one or several courses simply are not as reliable as averages based on grades in several courses for the same reason that tests with one or only a few items are not as reliable as total scores computed on many-item tests. We further wonder why (but are not critical that) grades earned during the first two years of undergraduate study and the number of semester hours of psychology were not included as predictors.

STUDENT RESPONSE. "Doesn't the regression phenomena enter in here? One presumes a 2.75 or 2.8 cut-off so you'd be looking mainly at very high grades to start with."

OUR REPLY. The subjects are a select, extreme group whose performance on measures other than undergraduate GPA is expected to regress toward more average levels. Because this group is not being compared with other groups, however, this regression effect is not a source of bias. The student does suggest a reason why undergraduate grades (and other measures used in student selection) might not be as highly related to the criteria as one would hope. Presumably the 42 subjects in the study all had quite good undergraduate grades (or else they would likely not have been admitted to graduate school). A predictor which does not discriminate among the students (that is, on which the students' performances are relatively homogeneous) is not likely to correlate highly with a criterion. Had all the students who applied to the doctorate program been admitted, regardless of their undergraduate grades or aptitude test scores, the correlations involving these predictors would undoubtedly have been greater. To see why this is the case, consider three persons whose IQs are 110, 111, and 112. There is no predicting who would do best in college. If their IQs were 50, 100, and 150 (mentally retarded, average, and gifted), making correct predictions would be easy.

(d)   Quality of Undergraduate Institution

Because grades at different institutions are not comparable, we see the inclusion of this variable as a wise decision both in studying its relationship with the criteria directly, and as a variable to use in adjusting undergraduate grade averages. More information about the number, nature, procedures, and criteria used by the committee to arrive at the quality ratings would be helpful to the reader who might wish to use the same variable in a local prediction study. Failure to specify fully how this variable was measured makes it of limited use to others.

Further, we wonder if the judges' ratings of particular institutions could have been biased by knowledge of which students came from which institutions. The judge, for example, might think more highly of institution X because student A, who is given high ratings on the "success" criteria, came from that institution. Conversely, perhaps students coming from institutions thought highly of were expected to do well and a self-fulfilling prophecy was in operation. This latter possible explanation for the positive correlation between the quality of undergraduate institution and most measures of "success" was noted by the investigator. As one student put it: "It looks like a case of circular reasoning. What schools are rated excellent? Those whose students do well at this university. And what students are successful at this university? Those who come from schools that are rated excellent! Shall we go another round?"

STUDENT RESPONSES. "There should be categories between 1 and 2 and between 2 and 3 which many schools would fit into more fairly and accurately." "The 3-point scale range is too small as to make the differences practically useless."

OUR REPLY. We disagree. Even 2-point scales (such as above average, below average) have been found to be very useful in predicting criteria. Although we certainly have no objection to a finer scale, the experience has been that added scale values result in rather meager gains in predictability.

4.   QUESTION:

The criteria of *short* term "success" are divided into three groups:

(a)   Grades earned in first year of graduate school
(b)   Self-report measures
(c)   Faculty ratings

Evaluate the appropriateness of the specific measures used in each of these groups of criteria. In your answer, focus upon whether these measures were reasonable choices and not whether, in fact, they related to the long-term "success" criterion.

4.   ANSWER:

(a)   Grades Earned in First Year Graduate School

(b) Self-Report Measures

(c) Faculty Ratings

4. ANSWER:

(a) Grades Earned in First Year Graduate School

Grades have typically been used as measures of success. It is a good idea to include them both because they are considered important and because they can be used to study their relationship to long-term success. We believe the investigators were wise to separate out the grades earned in core courses, for at least these grades would be comparable among the students. One student's grade in physiological psychology and another's grade in abnormal psychology, for example, might not be comparable. The fact that these core courses were included in the end-of-year average means that this composite measure will have a built-in dependency (correlation) with the other criteria in this category.

(b) Self-Report Measures

These two measures seem to be reasonable indicators of speed and persistence toward achieving the Ph.D.

STUDENT RESPONSES. "Why was the student rating expressed as slow or fast progress to a Ph.D. rather than feeling of satisfaction with progress whatever the speed?" "A student can be deeply engrossed in his study for learning's sake and be highly successful and motivated and yet be totally unconcerned with his speed toward his Ph.D. It is unfortunate that large universities often place the degree above the actual learning taking place."

OUR REPLY. Of course, other student self-report measures could have been used. We suspect that administrators and professors associated with the degree program were more concerned about the students' perceptions of their actual progress than these students' feelings of satisfaction about their progress. Since the investigators did include grades earned in first year graduate school among the criteria, "actual learning" was not ignored in this study.

STUDENT RESPONSE. "Self-report measures should not be obtained after the grades were issued, but before."

OUR REPLY. We found this to be an interesting reaction to which we could both agree and disagree. By requiring the student to report his progress before he receives the formal grades, we can obtain a measure of how he truly thought he was progressing and such an evaluation might be less contaminated by faculty opinion. On the other hand, by permitting the student access to the formal grades as information to use in making a considered judgment of his progress, a more realistic estimate of his true progress might result.

(c) Faculty Ratings

Such categories as, "excellent progress, assured of financial aid," and, "dropped from graduate program," simply do not seem to be points on a common scale. These ratings appear to encompass a whole gamut of possibilities, including good performance, persistence, and voluntary withdrawal, and we would like to have seen all of the scale values for these ratings. Further, the shorthand labels of these variables in Tables 1 and 2 do not seem especially appropriate.

STUDENT RESPONSE. Many students felt that, "there could be bias in a faculty member's opinion," and that faculty ratings, ". . . are an unfair criterion." Further, many students wanted, ". . . to know how divergent the various faculty members were in the rating of the same student."

OUR REPLY. We agree that faculty ratings might have bias and not be a fair rating of a student's real progress. In addition, as one student pointed out, ". . . faculty ratings can be influenced by predictor ratings." (We discussed this a bit toward the end of our answer to Question 3d above.) Since each student's faculty ratings were averages of several ratings, the influence of a single professor's bias or susceptability to contamination by a predictor was lessened. We, too, wanted to know how closely the faculty agreed in their ratings. Although we recognize faculty ratings will have at least some shortcomings, we nevertheless support the use of faculty ratings as a criterion of short-term success. The fact that the hiring of recent Ph.D.s depends heavily on the recommendations of the students' professors serves to remind us that colleges and universities consider such faculty ratings to be a suitable criterion.

5. QUESTION:

A key concept in this study is "long-term success."

A. Give two or more reasons for rejecting the definition given this term in the section, Long-Term Criterion, on Page 52.
B. How might this definition be defended?

5. ANSWER:

A. Before listing many objections to the definition of long-term success, it is necessary to point out a confusion on the part of several students. The professors of the students did NOT make the long-term success ratings. Rather, these professors were asked only to define what they thought "constitutes 'success' for a psychology doctoral student." Based on these answers, the investigators, in some unexplained way, constructed the 9-point long-term success scale. Two judges (probably two of the investigators or their assistants) then made the rating using the information (*available at the time the student left the university*) of where the student was going and the "circumstances" of his leaving. Thus, for practically all students, the *long-term* success index was determined from data available well before six years had elapsed.

Probably the most serious criticism of the long-term success measure is that it fails to consider many factors commonly thought of as indicators of success. Not included, presumably, (presumably because we do not know the intermediate scale values), are such indicators as quality of teaching, service to the profession, grants awarded, number and quality of publications, and so forth. "Acceptance to a highly prestigious institution," is not usually thought of as the only or even the most valid indicator of long-term success. The incompleteness and irrelevance of the measure of long-term success is clearly the most serious flaw in the study.

Typical student comments which we included under this first objection are the following: "There seems to be little concern for the performance on the job in this research." "Those who drop out are automatically excluded from being judged successful." "It would be possible for a student to withdraw from the program and later continue the study of psychology and be successful."

Second, we believe that the success measure would be strengthened if it took into account at least the program from which each person graduated. For example, a long-term success measure for a graduate of the clinical program might be quite different from that for a graduate of an experimental psychology program.

Third, we agree with one student who pointed out that the investigators' *long-term* measure is, ". . . not measuring long-term success; it is merely rating a student as to the circumstances under which he left the University. To measure long-term success his career has to be followed up after he left." Other students worded this objection as follows: "Success cannot be measured immediately after graduation. Determination of long-term success must be made after a period of time has elapsed." "Notation was made of where a student *intended* to go but no follow-up on the students was made." "The 'long-term' success is not long enough. A person may have accepted a prestigious position, but may not have been able to retain it." "The use of the word long-term is unfortunate. The long term aspect of the question would deal with careers."

Fourth, it should be noted that the 9-point scale is not fully identified. We can only speculate as to what description (if any) is given to the intermediate points. As we indicated earlier in our discussion of ratings of short-term success (see our answer to Question 4c), the points on the long-term success scale do not seem to be tapping a common dimension. It is difficult to know where to place a person who, for example, drops out of a program but yet demonstrates "success" in other ways.

Fifth, as one student pointed out, "The definition may be rejected on the basis of the narrow sampling of experts used in determining what is and what is not success. They are professors at the same institution in the same department who are probably prone to similar thoughts on an issue such as this." The restricted nature of the sample (number not given) of faculty whose opinions were used in developing the long-term success scale increases the likelihood that the criterion will not seem appropriate to other faculty groups.

Finally, note a built-in dependency between short and long-term criteria. If a person drops out of graduate school he must necessarily receive a low rating on both the short-term and long-term assessment. Thus, the relationship between long-term and short-term criteria is almost predetermined even though the study of this relationship is presented as a primary objective of this research.

STUDENT RESPONSES. "With only two judges, what does a reliability of .95 mean?" "I have difficulty with the 'inter-judge reliability' which was .95 when there were only two judges."

OUR REPLY. The records of the 42 students were rated on the 9-point scale twice, once by each judge. The correlation coefficient computed on these 42 pairs of ratings was .95. These two judges agreed almost perfectly on the relative ratings assigned to the students. A reasonable inference is that the high agreement resulted from a clear definition of the scale points.

B. The senior author of the article, in personal communication, defended the definition of long-term success by writing: "*I* believe it is important to be able to predict things like which graduate students are most likely to flunk out *vs*. withdraw *vs*. get a Ph.D. and take a job at Podunk University *vs*. get a Ph.D. and accept a job at a prestigious university such as Cornell. Certainly the faculty of graduate schools feel that such 'long-term' criteria are important."

6. QUESTION:

Are investigators permitted to define key terms (such as "long-term success") any way they wish? Explain why you answered as you did.

6. ANSWER:

Our first three objections to the investigators' definition of "long-term success" (see our answer to Question 5A) suggest what we think the term to mean. In commenting on our critique, the senior author wrote us: "Long-term, which to us meant 'after the end of a student's graduate education' apparently implied some kind of career-long perspective to Messrs. Millman and Gowin. They can mean whatever they want to, but in discussing our study I'd suggest they talk about our *operational* measure (which indeed has some problems) rather than focus entirely on the name we put on our measure."

We would agree that investigators should be permitted to define their terms as they like. On the other hand, they do have an obligation to foster accurate communication about their work and this goal is not sufficiently achieved when labels are used which convey meanings markedly different from those intended. In such situations, it is often possible to be misled into thinking that accounts of a study are more generalizable and significant than they actually are because persuasive labels (such as "long-term success") are given meanings unintended by the author.

7. QUESTION:

A student reviewer of this study stated that this investigation merely demonstrates what was already common knowledge. Do you agree? Support your answer.

7. ANSWER:

We disagree. We were surprised, for example, that the investigators found negative correlations between undergraduate grades and their "global assessment of success" rating. In spite of our misgivings about this "long-term success" index we would have anticipated at least small positive correlations. Further, we would not have expected rated quality of institution to be such a good predictor of long-term success. Many readers would not have predicted these findings, and hence they could not be considered common knowledge.

STUDENT RESPONSES. "I thought that facility in a foreign language would be a great asset towards long-term success in doctoral studies." "I was surprised that GRE-Quantitative and GPA mathematics correlated .00." "I didn't expect there to be so many negative correlations."

OUR REPLY. There is probably very little that is common knowledge. Like beauty, surprise is in the eyes of the beholder.

8. QUESTION:

Question 8a. through 8d. are based upon the following sentence quoted from column two on page 54:

> For example, the quality of the undergraduate school, which predicted first-year grades negligibly, was found to be significantly related to student

and faculty global assessments of progress toward the Ph.D. at the end of the year, and correlated more substantially with the long-term criterion of success.

Look again at the tables in the report of the study.

8a. QUESTION:

Find those numbers which indicate the degree of relationship between quality of the undergraduate school and the other variables mentioned in the quotation. What numerical values of correlations did the investigators find to lead them to make their statement which is quoted above?

8a. ANSWER:

From the last line of Table 1, the "negligible" correlations between rated quality of undergraduate school and graduate school grades are: .00, −.13, .21, .16, and .15. The significant relations to students and faculty ratings of *progress* toward the degree are .30 and .31, also found in the last line of Table 1. The same line also shows a .43 correlation with the long-term measure of success.

8b. QUESTION:

Can a negligible correlation be statistically significant from zero?

8b. ANSWER:

Yes. Some people would say that for prediction purposes the significant correlations referred to in the quotation of .30 and .31 are negligible. The "negligible" correlation of .21 would be statistically significant if 88 instead of 42 students were involved in the study. Correlations of .30 and .31 would not be significant at the $4\frac{1}{2}\%^2$ level of significance. We wish to make two points: (1) In this context, negligible is an adjective describing the *magnitude* of a correlation; significance describes a different attribute

---

[2] Arrived at by a t test of the significance of a correlation from zero.

—the likelihood of correlations of a given value occurring in a random sample of a population in which the actual correlation is zero. All four combinations of these two descriptive adjectives are possible: negligible, significant; negligible, not significant; not negligible, significant; not negligible, not significant. (2) One must be careful not to have an unthinking attachment to correlations (or other statistical indices) which are barely statistically significant at some level of confidence, and distain for correlations which do not quite make the cut-off between significant and not significant. (Note our answer to Question 8d.)

8c. QUESTION:

For these 42 students, which pre-enrollment predictor was able to predict the long-term global assessment criterion most accurately? On what evidence do you base your answer?

8c. ANSWER:

Undergraduate GPA in the physical sciences is the best predictor. The correlations between the pre-enrollment predictors and the long-term success criterion are given in the last column of Table 1. GPA in the physical sciences has the highest correlation $(-.50)$ and, thus, would predict the criterion best. Because the correlation is negative, students having a *low* GPA in physical science would be predicted to have the *highest* long-term success rating and vice versa. The predictor having the highest *positive* relation with the long-term success criterion is, as the investigators state in the sentence quoted, quality of the undergraduate school.

8d. QUESTION:

If the appropriate statistical test were run, guess whether the quality of the undergraduate school would correlate with the long-term success criterion *significantly* more (in the statistical sense) than, say, the quantitative score on the GRE?

8d. ANSWER:

This difference is *not* statistically significant. It is true that both cor-relations are significantly *different from zero* at the 5% level. This fact is indicated by the asterisks affixed to the correlations of .32 and .43 in the last column of Table 1. The point being illustrated is that correlations which are significantly different from zero need not be, and indeed frequently are not, significantly different from each other. A clear-cut example might be two correlations of .80 and .79 being each significantly different from zero but having a difference (.01) that is not significant. The investigators did not test the difference *between* correlations in any of the tables and state-ments comparing the relative sizes of them should be made cautiously.[3]

9. QUESTION:

One of the findings of the study, as pointed out in Question 8 above is that rated quality of undergraduate institution has a fairly high correlation with long-term success. Does this mean that if you were an admissions offi-cer in the Psychology Department at the University of Illinois and pri-marily interested in this measurement of success you should give preference to students coming from highly rated undergraduate institutions? Why or why not?

9. ANSWER:

If, and this is a big if, you were interested in predicting this long-term success measure, then yes, you should give preference to students coming from undergraduate institutions rated high by the same (vaguely described) procedures used in this study. (Quality of undergraduate school should not be the only factor considered, of course.) It is true that this high correlation may not show up in another sample, but chances are better that the vari-able will be positively related than that the relationship will disappear. The existence of a high correlation between quality of undergraduate insti-tution and long-term success does not mean that the quality of undergradu-ate institution *caused* the students to have long-term success—indeed, the same forces which are responsible for a student's selecting (or being selected

---

[3] A procedure for testing differences between these correlations is described on page 158 of Quinn McNemar, *Psychological Statistics,* 4th ed. (New York: John Wiley, 1969).

by) a highly rated institution might be operating at the time he selects (or is being selected by) his employer upon his graduation.

STUDENT RESPONSES. "I would not give any preference to those students coming from a highly rated institution. What a person puts into an institution is what he will get out of it." "Absolutely not. To me the entire record should be evaluated and equal weight given to all variables, insuring fairness and a chance for the student to achieve this goal if he really has the desire to try." "As an admission officer in the Psychology Department at the University of Illinois, I wouldn't show a preference to students coming from highly rated undergraduate institutions. I would, however, carefully consider all information in the folders of all applicants." "The GREs would be important to me as a comparison of the individual students so this would definitely affect my decision." "I would not give any preference to students coming from highly rated institutions. The rating scale was too narrow and biased."

OUR REPLY. The above comments of student readers appear to be a denial of the facts, namely that the quality of undergraduate institution was predictive of the long-term success measure. The rating scale may indeed be narrow and biased, but it worked. Most of the other information in the folders, particularly undergraduate grades and some GRE scores, have either low or negative correlations with the success measure or unknown predictive validity for this criterion. That is, there is not sufficient evidence to believe that these other variables will be effective in predicting the student who will be rated high on the long-term success measure. One can find good reasons for objecting to the appropriateness of this criterion, but that is not the issue under consideration. (Reread Question 9.)

STUDENT RESPONSES. "It is more likely that strong individuals are selected by high quality institutions. Therefore, the judgment should be made on the basis of the individual and not the institution." "The long-term 'success' of students coming from highly rated undergraduate institutions may be due in part to the self-fulfilling prophecy. Students coming from a highly rated undergraduate institution may get hired by prestigious universities because such universities may expect them to do well merely on the basis of this undergraduate school."

OUR REPLY. The student who made the first response overlooks the fact that it was the institution and not the "individual" predictors that worked. Both students, and many other readers whose responses we did not quote, quite properly attempted to explain the reason for the success of the undergraduate institution quality rating as a predictor.

STUDENT RESPONSE. "Students must be selected for more justifiable reasons than what the names of their undergraduate schools were. A better measure must be found."

OUR REPLY. In this student-reader comment the frustration of many of us is given expression. One student discussed the dilemma in these words:

Being intelligent, perceptive, and liberal, I, of course, would not discriminate against a student from a low-rated school. However, if I had to *bet* on which student would succeed, I would go with a student from a high-rated school. These statistics indicate I would have a better chance of winning.

An example of another area of concern may help to clarify the situation. Suppose you own a company that produces screws and nuts (metal variety)! The more screws and nuts turned out by an employee, the more money you, as a company owner, will earn. Your personnel office reports a company study in which, let us assume, race correlates .43 with production —white employees producing more per man hour than black employees. Now, you know that skin color *per se* is not the cause of this differential production, and that there is some more basic reason. But, while you ponder the underlying causes, a vacancy occurs and two people, one black and the other white, apply for the job. The applicants are equal on all other factors you usually consider. Whom do you choose? If money is the only criterion you would "bet" on the white man. If, as company owner, you are willing to consider more unselfish motives relating to, say, society's needs, you might give the black applicant a chance.

None of the predictors in the present graduate school study tells the whole story; and they may well discriminate against the poor, the late bloomer, and the special student. An admissions officer may try to be fair to such people by deviating from total reliance on the best predictors available to him by choosing individuals with a lower probability of success. When he does so, it is because he feels that criteria other than his success measures are important. Of all institutions, educational ones are perhaps best able to afford using multiple indicators of success.

It would certainly be nice if each person could, ". . . be given the chance to fail or to succeed on his own without a survey telling him he can or cannot do it." When demand greatly exceeds supply (e.g., only some of the applicants to graduate school can be admitted), not everyone can be given that chance, and choices have to be made.

6

The Influence of Analysis
and Evaluation Questions
on Achievement
in Sixth Grade Social Studies*

Francis P. Hunkins

INTRODUCTION

Questions used by teachers in their discourse and those incorporated in instructional materials probably are significant in guiding the development of pupils' levels of knowledge and achievement. Questions reveal the operational objectives which stress, for example, the increase of pupils' knowledge of facts, of understandings, of concepts, and of pupils' skills at interpreting information and ideas.

The classroom teacher devotes a large portion of his time to asking questions, e.g., Adams (1), Aschner (2), Barr (3), Floyd (7), Stevens (9). The usefulness of questions has long been recognized as significant in the teaching-learning interaction. Yet, even with this

* Originally appeared in Educational Leadership Research Supplement, January 1968, pp. 326–332. Reprinted with permission of the Association for Supervision and Curriculum Development and Francis P. Hunkins. Copyright © 1968 by the Association for Supervision and Curriculum Development.

purported awareness of the importance of questions, little has been done with regard to the effects questions have upon pupils' achievement within the class situation.

This research was concerned with determining the relative effectiveness of knowledge, analysis, and evaluation questions in stimulating achievement in sixth grade social studies. These question types were based on three of the six hierarchical categories of Benjamin Bloom's *Taxonomy of Educational Objectives*, Bloom (4).

CRITICS' NOTE:

The Taxonomy of Educational Objectives **is a book by Benjamin Bloom and others in which are described types of cognitive abilities organized into the following categories: knowledge, comprehension, application, analysis, synthesis, and evaluation. Each of these categories is further subdivided into more specific skills and abilities. The authors of this** volume hypothesize that these six major categories are hierarchically arranged with knowledge at the bottom of the scale and evaluation at the top, and with each step of the scale dependent upon mastery of previous categories. Thus, for example, they hypothesize that an individual cannot properly evaluate (category 6) a statement about, say, atoms without first learning certain facts about atoms (1), comprehending certain ideas about them (2), being able to analyze these facts and ideas (4), and so on.

Knowledge questions require the recall of ideas, facts, materials, or phenomena. They call for the releasing of certain information stored in the individual's memory. Analysis questions, on the other hand, demand the arrangement and rearrangement of information into elements, relationships, and organizations. The third type of question, evaluation, requires a judgment employing criteria such as accuracy, effectiveness, economic quality, or satisfying quality. These two latter question types subsume knowledge. The evaluation type of question subsumes both knowledge and analysis.

OBJECTIVES

This study sought to determine whether a dominant use in social studies text-type materials of analysis and evaluation questions, as defined by Bloom's *Taxonomy*, would effectively stimulate the development of sixth grade pupils' social studies achievement. The overall hypothesis tested, stated in null form was:

Use of text-type materials employing questions requiring "analysis" and "evaluation" will not result in differences in sixth grade pupils' social studies achievement when compared with the use of text-type materials incorporating questions requiring the recall of knowledge in relationship to pupils' (a) reading level, (b) sex, and (c) the interaction between these variables.

GENERAL PLAN OF THE STUDY

The general plan of the study first involved constructing two sets of text-type materials and corresponding answer sheets, one set stressing questions requiring analysis and evaluation (Condition A) and the other stressing questions requiring knowledge (Condition B). Pupils in both treatment conditions were directed to read designated sections of their textbook and to respond in writing to the questions on their worksheets.

For four weeks, pupils used these materials during a thirty-five minute portion of the daily social studies period. For this study, the instructional unit dealt with Africa and Oceania and was based on chapters in the adopted social studies textbook used by the cooperating school system. The general format and directions of the two sets of special materials were identical, the only varying factor being the questions and their emphases. During the experimental period, teachers refrained from actively engaging in teaching but assisted in coordinating the pupils' use of the materials. This lack of active teacher participation was an attempt to reduce their influence on the experimental situation.

PROCEDURE

Subjects

Two hundred and sixty pupils served as subjects in this study. They were enrolled in eleven sixth grade classes in three elementary schools serving the same geographic area of a large suburban public school system in a northeastern Ohio community (population, 47,922, 1960 census). The eleven classes were randomly assigned to one of two experimental treatment conditions, A or B. A total of 127 pupils (67 boys and 60 girls) were assigned to Condition A, while 133 pupils (55 boys and 78 girls) were assigned to Condition B. Background data were collected and analyzed for both pupils and teachers.

Intelligence quotients were obtained from the *California Test of Mental Maturity*, S Form. The mean IQ for boys in Treatment A was 114.84, SD 16.06 (N = 67). Girls in the same treatment had a mean IQ of 115.80, SD 15.10, (N = 60). In Treatment B, the mean IQ for boys was 112.07, SD 15.38 (N = 55), and the mean IQ for girls was 113.11, SD of 12.65 (N = 78).

Reading test scores were obtained on the subjects from the *Stanford Achievement Test,* Form W. Boys in Treatment A had a mean reading score of 38.90, SD 12.18; girls in the same treatment had a mean reading score of 41.86, SD 11.45. Boys in Treatment B had a mean reading score of 36.45, SD 10.39, while girls in the same treatment had a mean reading score of 39.29, SD 9.74.

Pupils' IQ scores and reading scores were subjected to analysis of variance to determine if significant differences were present. For this analysis, scores were considered across reading levels by treatment and sex.

No significant differences in IQ were revealed between the two treatments, between boys and girls, or their interaction. Thus IQ was eliminated as a possible covariant on subsequent analyses of the criterion data. No significant differences between reading achievement were noted between the two treatments and no significant interaction either. A significant difference between the reading scores of boys and girls was observed. However, this relationship was not considered sufficient reason to use the reading scores as covariants on subsequent analyses of criterion data. Had significant differences in reading achievement existed between

treatments, such scores would have been employed as covariants.

Background data on the participating teachers revealed that teachers of classes in both conditions were similar with respect to age and teaching experience.

The mean age for teachers with pupils involved in Treatment A was 35.16, while the mean age for those teachers with pupils involved in Treatment B was 33.20. Experience in teaching was similar, with means of 8.33 years for teachers in Treatment A and 8.80 years for teachers in Treatment B. The Treatment A teachers had slightly more years in teaching the sixth grade, mean 5.66 years, than did the teachers in Treatment B, mean 3.80 years. Ten of the eleven teachers involved had Bachelor degrees. The one teacher without the degree, in Treatment A, had over 24 years of teaching experience. Of the total teacher group, only one teacher had a Master's degree, in Treatment B.

Collection of Data

A criterion test of achievement covering the selected social studies unit was constructed by the investigator. The objective of the test design was to afford a single achievement score in addition to six subscores corresponding to the six categories in Bloom's *Taxonomy*: knowledge, comprehension, application, analysis, synthesis, and evaluation. However, only the total achievement score was of concern in this phase of the investigation.

A total of 59 multiple-choice, four option items was written and submitted to two judges well-acquainted with the *Taxonomy*. With four exceptions, only items having 100 percent agreement among the judges and investigator regarding *Taxonomy* emphasis were selected for the final test which contained 42 items. The test contained seven questions in each of the six Bloom categories. Reliability of the post-test was determined to be .68 using the Kuder-Richardson formula. This reliability is quite low and the reader should bear this in mind when considering the results.

Experimental Material and Procedure

Pupils in both experimental treatments used the regularly adopted social studies text, *The Changing Old World*, by Cooper, Sorensen, and Todd (5). The unit for study during the experiment was "Africa, Australia and New Zealand." This unit was deemed appropriate, for the investigator felt that the subjects would not bring abundant prior knowledge into the experimental situation.

EXPERIMENTAL PUPIL MATERIALS. For each experimental treatment condition, special materials and answer sheets were constructed. The sets for both conditions were identical in format and directions. Seventeen sets for each condition were developed to correspond to discrete portions of the adopted text. Both treatment groups experienced an identical introductory set to familiarize them with the materials. Condition A materials had 47.53 percent of the total questions in the analysis and evaluation categories: 28.41 percent analysis, and 19.12 percent evaluation. Condition B materials contained a question emphasis on knowledge of 87.38 percent of the total number.

These materials had been submitted to the same judges who served to classify the achievement test items. Every question of each set was categorized by the judges, and following this, the two individuals met with the investigator to compare results. If a question emphasis could not be agreed upon after discussion, the question was either rewritten until the desired emphasis was obtained or not employed in the final draft of the materials. This procedure was followed in order to ascertain that these question emphases did exist.

A readability analysis, employing the Dale-Chall formula, Dale and Chall (6), was used to determine the reading level of both the experimental materials and the answer sheets in both Conditions A and B. Results of this analysis revealed that the experimental materials had an average raw score of 5.64, designating a reading level well within the range of fifth and sixth grade pupils. Analysis of the answer sheets revealed an average raw score of 5.65, also designating the material as appropriate for sixth graders.

WORKING WITH THE MATERIALS. Pupils in both conditions were instructed to work independently with the materials. They were given from 30 to 35 minutes each day to work with the experimental sets, reading carefully and writing their answers in the provided spaces. Pupils were provided time to check their work with the answer sheets.

ANALYSIS OF DATA

The experimental design basic to this study was an analysis of covariance design. Within each treatment condition, data were analyzed according to sex and reading achievement. This resulted in a $2 \times 2 \times 4$ (treatment $\times$ sex $\times$ reading level) classificatory scheme. Pupils were assigned reading levels according to quartile ranks as determined by their raw scores on the reading achievement test (*Stanford Achievement Test*, Form W). The four levels had the following ranges: Quartile 1, 0–31; Quartile 2, 32–38; Quartile 3, 39–47; and Quartile 4, 48–64.

CRITICS' NOTE:

The investigator incorrectly uses the word "quartile" to mean quarter. The first *quartile* is 31.5, the point below which 25% of the scores lie. The first *quarter* of scores covers the range 0 through 31.

Table 1
Summary of Analysis of Covariance of Post-test Scores on Achievement Test

Sourse of Variation	Original		Adjusted			
	d.f.	S.S.	d.f.	S.S.	M.S.	F
Treatment	1	12.06	1	10.05	10.05	9.85**
Reading level	3	133.55	3	65.02	21.67	21.24**
Sex	1	.92	1	.92	.92	.90
Treatment × reading level	3	.49	3	.23	.07	.06
Treatment × sex	1	.75	1	.26	.26	.25
Reading level × sex	3	2.29	3	.63	.21	.20
Treatment × reading level × sex	3	8.06	3	7.21	2.40	2.35
Within groups	244	269.88	243	247.98	1.02	

** Significant at the .01 level.

RESULTS

The post-test achievement scores were subjected to analysis of covariance adjusting for the pre-achievement scores. These results are summarized in Table 1.

No statistically significant differences in achievement between boys and girls were observed, and there were no significant interactions. Condition A pupils achieved more than did Condition B pupils, and better readers obtained higher achievement scores than did poorer readers.

The means for between reading levels were contrasted by a series of t tests, all of which revealed statistically significant differences $(Q_4 > Q_3 > Q_2 > Q_1)$. It appears from these data that whether one can handle high-level questions is related to how well one can read. The higher-level questions usually were more involved with regard to wording than were the knowledge questions. Also, it should be borne in mind that both worksheets and answer sheets placed demands upon pupils' reading skills.

CONCLUSIONS

From the analyses conducted, the following conclusions are warranted:

1. The employment of high cognitive-level questions (analysis and evaluation) produced significantly greater scores in social studies achievement than did low cognitive-level questions (knowledge).

2. Better readers in both conditions achieved higher than did poorer readers.

As a result of these significant differences, the major null hypothesis relating to social studies achievement was rejected.

CRITICS' NOTE:

Recall from the design that there were two treatments (Condition A in which questions requiring analysis and evaluation were stressed, and Condition B in which questions requiring only knowledge were in the majority), four reading levels, and the two sexes. Each student was considered to fall into one of these 16 possible categories (i.e., 2 × 4 × 2 = 16). One category, for example, would be Condition A, reading level 2, girl.

Table 1 shows the results of a statistical analysis designed to test if there were significant differences in achievement scores among students in certain combinations of the categories. In each of the first seven *rows* of the table are reported the results of an analysis involving a different such comparison. The *Source of Variation* column identifies the comparisons involved. By *Treatment* is meant the comparison between Condition A and Condition B, or more precisely, between the scores of students in the eight categories involving Condition A with the scores of students in the eight categories involving Condition B. Similarly, the reading level comparison involves a test of the significance of the differences among the scores of students in the four reading level conditions. If boys score significantly higher than girls (or vice versa), it will be reflected in the results of the sex comparison shown in row three. By statistically significant is meant that the differences are sufficiently large that it is unlikely that they could occur by random sampling, or by chance alone.

The next four rows involve interaction comparisons. Since these interaction effects were neither significant nor of much concern in this study, they will not be discussed further here. The concept of interaction is discussed in regard to other articles in this series.

The last effect represents differences in scores among the students within each of the 16 categories. These differences are not tested for significance; rather they serve as a base from which to evaluate the other differences associated with the first seven effects.

The investigator performed two kinds of analyses—one involving the actual achievement scores and the other involving scores that were "adjusted" for pre-test score differences. In both cases, the *d.f.* column represents degrees of freedom which relate to (but do not exactly equal) the number of groups being compared. The *S.S.* columns and the *M.S.* column stand for the sum of squares and mean square respectively, and are intermediate calculations in the analysis of variance.

The numbers in the *F* column are used to indicate if results are statistically significant. For a given number of degrees of freedom (*d.f.*), the higher the *F* number the *un*likely that chance alone could account for the differences, and the more statistically significant the results. You will note that the difference in test scores (when adjusted for pre-achievement score differences) of students in Conditions A and B, and of students in the four reading conditions, were statistically significant.

DISCUSSION

Analysis of the data suggests that questions requiring analysis and evaluation stimulated individuals to utilize general viewpoints regarding the information embedded in the task. It seems reasonable that pupils, using such questions, might have been forced to engage in the intellectual activity of considering various aspects of factual knowledge and evaluating the complexity, implications, and applications of such knowledge. Such mental "juggling" may have enabled pupils to know better the information with which they were dealing.

It is assumed that high-level questions will demand of individuals more intellectual activity than would be true with low-level questions. Since the data revealed a significantly greater achievement among the pupils receiving such high-level questions, one might cautiously conclude that the pupils did in fact react more actively with information presented. The evidence seems to suggest, rather than confirm, that pupils were engaged in an interaction with the materials presented. Analysis of the sub-tests of the achievement test, presently being conducted in a second phase of the research, may provide evidence to clarify somewhat exactly how the high-level questions affected various dimensions of achievement.

That the evidence is suggestive rather than confirming should not be cause for alarm. This research is a beginning, not a conclusion regarding the effects of questions. It is premature to make definite statements. These types of questions do have the potential, it seems, to make pupils uneasy, but also to encourage them to probe their knowledge and to discover meanings.

IMPLICATIONS OF THE STUDY

Several implications may be drawn from this study regarding the role of questions in relation to social studies achievement in particular and overall school achievement in general. If questions at higher-cognitive levels are capable of stimulating high achievement, then teachers should be using these questions in much greater numbers than they currently do. Teachers, by improving their level of questioning, could very well make information more meaningful for their pupils. In addition, pupils in classrooms where high-level questions are used by teachers should be expected to employ such questions themselves when they engage in class discussions and other class work. Higher-level questions not only should stimulate higher levels of achievement, but also should make pupils better inquirers into the realm of knowledge.

REFERENCES

1. THOMAS HOWARD ADAMS. *The Development of a Method for Analysis of Questions Asked by Teachers in Classroom Discourse.* Doctor's thesis. New Brunswick, New Jersey: Rutgers, The State University, 1964. 149 pp.

2. MARY JANE McCUE ASCHNER. "Asking Questions to Trigger Think-

ing." *NEA Journal* 50 (6); 44–46; September 1961.

3. A. S. BARR. *Characteristic Differences in the Teaching Performance of Good and Poor Teachers of the Social Studies.* Bloomington, Illinois: Public School Publishing Co., 1929. 127 pp.

4. BENJAMIN S. BLOOM, editor. *Taxonomy of Educational Objectives The Classification of Educational Goals: Handbook I Cognitive Domain.* New York: David McKay Company, Inc., 1956. 207 pp.

5. KENNETH S. COOPER, CLARENCE W. SORENSEN, and LEWIS PAUL TODD. *The Changing Old World.* Morristown, New Jersey: Silver Burdett Company, Inc., 1961. 470 pp.

6. EDGAR DALE, and JEANNE S. CHALL. "A Formula for Predicting Readability." *Educational Research Bulletin* 27: 11–20, 28; January 1948. 27: 37–54; February 1948.

7. WILLIAM D. FLOYD. *An Analysis of the Oral Questioning Activity in Selected Colorado Primary Classrooms.* Doctor's thesis. Greeley: Colorado State College, 1960. 195 pp.

8. FRANK M. GATTO. *Pupils Questions: Their Nature and Their Relationship to the Study Process.* Doctor's thesis. Pittsburgh, Pennsylvania: University of Pittsburgh, 1928. 158 pp.

9. ROMIETT STEVENS. *The Question as a Measure of Efficiency in Instruction.* Teachers College Contribution to Education. No. 48. New York: Teachers College, Columbia University, 1912. 95 pp.

10. SOSHICHI YAMADA. "A Study of Questioning." *Pedagogical Seminar* 20: 129–85; 1913.

CRITIQUE

1. QUESTION:

Do you think the title a good one? Why?

1. ANSWER:

A good title for a research report will describe the contents of that report as accurately and as completely and concisely as possible. This particular study is an investigation of the effects of several kinds of questions asked upon subsequent achievement. The written materials used and questions asked dealt with social studies; the grade level was sixth; relationships with reading level and sex were investigated as well as teacher differences and pretest scores for students. Not all of these elements can be easily mentioned in a title and therefore the investigator must choose those he considers most essential for inclusion.

Not clear from the title was that the principal independent variable was the kind of question asked and answer provided. A better (but not the best) title would have been, "A Comparison between Knowledge and Higher-level Questions and Answers on Achievement in Sixth Grade Social Studies." But other than this concern that a description of the manipulated variable be given priority in the title, we think the title a fairly good one.

Some students objected to the use of the word "influence" in the title and felt that the study was inconclusive and influence was not demonstrated. We do *not* share this concern because a title need not convey the specific finding, only the intended problem. Thus, a study with a title that begins, "The Relationship between . . ." might have as its finding that there is no relationship between the variables investigated. Although titles such as "A Study of the Influence of . . ." and "An Investigation of the Relationship between . . ." would be less ambiguous, it is accepted practice to use the abbreviated version.

2. QUESTION:

Reread the introductory section if you need to refresh your memory.

Does this research provide a test of the hierarchical hypothesis implicit in the Bloom *et al.* taxonomy? Give reasons for your answer. (See the Critics' Note on pages 74–75 for a discussion of this hypothesis.)

2. ANSWER:

The study does not *prove* the hierarchical hypothesis is true; nor does the investigator claim that it does. Since only three levels are involved, this research cannot provide a complete test of the hierarchical nature of all six levels. Further, just because the research is *"concerned"* with Bloom's taxonomy does not mean it provides a test of it. Whether the study even gives *some* support for it is a question about which experts disagree. Some say NO and argue that the hierarchical hypothesis is assumed to be correct and merely used as a starting point about which the research is organized. Others say YES and argue that the results are consistent with the hierarchical hypothesis and thus give some support for its validity.

A lesson to be learned from this specific question and answer is that a criterion for a hypothesis to be tested is the presence of data which can count as evidence in support of or against the hypothesis. Those who answered YES should be able to point out such evidence. The personal views expressed by many students that the hypothesis is most reasonable and that the distinctions among the cognitive levels are very important do not, in themselves, justify the conclusion that the hypothesis was being tested by the research.

3. QUESTION:

Reread the section entitled "Objectives" if you need to refresh your memory. Do you think the overall hypothesis is a clear and accurate statement of the hypothesis the investigator wishes to test?

3. ANSWER:

The statement is probably quite accurate, although awkwardly phrased. We would have preferred deletion of the ending: "in relationship to . . . ." A separate sentence could have been added to describe these scondary concerns.

We might note that the standard procedure is to express the hypotheses in the direction the investigator really expects them to be true, rather than in the "null" form used. The use of the null form is not incorrect, but it does represent unsophisticated reporting. It is the substantive question (hypothesis) the reader wants to know about.

4. QUESTION:

Reread the section "General Plan of the Study" if you need to refresh your memory.

4a. QUESTION:

Did the investigator construct the materials about Africa and Oceania? Give reasons for your answer.

4a. ANSWER:

It is true that, ". . . two sets of text-type materials . . . ," were constructed by the investigator. However, these sets stressed questions and must have been widely supplemented by other materials, primarily the textbook. Note that "Pupils in both treatment conditions were directed to read designated sections of their textbooks. . . ." We believe the special instructional materials constructed by the investigator consisted only of questions and answers.

4b. QUESTION:

Were the questions used in the *instruction* of the multiple-choice type? Give reasons for your answer.

4b. ANSWER:

No, at least not all the questions used in *instruction* were of this type. Note that the pupils had, ". . . to respond in writing to the questions on their worksheets." This suggests that students had to *construct* their responses rather than simply *select* their responses as is the case with multiple-choice questions. Do not confuse the criterion test of achievement, which did consist of multiple-choice questions, with the questions asked as part of the instruction.

4c. QUESTION:

The investigator attempted to reduce the influence of the teacher on the experimental situation by avoiding active teacher participation. Was this wise? Give reasons for your answer.

4c. ANSWER:

Yes and no. By reducing teacher participation, the investigator can be more certain that the differences in scores of students using the two sets of materials are actually due to the experimental variable "type of question asked." We say that the study is more likely to have *internal* validity. However, the price paid for this internal validity is a lessening of the *external* validity because the study results may be reliably applied to limited classroom practices.[1] By minimizing the role of the teacher we cannot determine what the effects might be if teachers asked the different types of questions rather than presenting them in written form alone. The investigator has gained control at the expense of conducting the investigation under fairly narrow and less typical conditions. Many research experts argue, as

---

[1] For a discussion of internal and external validity, read Donald T. Campbell and Julian C. Stanley, *Experimental and Quasi-experimental Designs for Research* (Skokie, Ill.: Rand McNally, 1966).

this investigator evidently does, that it is more important to guarantee that the comparisons made are valid even though this validity necessitates confining the research to a study of less typical practices. But compromises must be made and we certainly do not fault the investigator for restricting the role of the teacher.

5. QUESTION:

Reread the section entitled "Subjects" if you need to refresh your memory.

5a. QUESTION:

Note that the proportion of boys to girls (67:60) in Condition A does not equal the proportion (55:78) in Condition B. Does this fact mean that the comparison on the criterion achievement test between students in Conditions A and B is misleading? Why?

5a. ANSWER:

Unless controlled for in the analysis, a comparison between all the students in the two conditions would be misleading if boys and girls do not perform equally on the dependent variable. Since performance on the criterion test is related to reading ability, and since the girls in this study were reported to be better readers than the boys, it is not unreasonable, therefore, to expect that on this basis boys and girls will score differently on the criterion test. Thus, condition B with a higher proportion of girls, could have an unfair advantage. As it turned out, such bias is of little concern since Condition A was still judged to be superior to Condition B in spite of the possible advantage given to the latter treatment.

One way to control for these differences is to report criterion test scores separately for boys and girls. Another way is to weigh equally each of the 16 subcategories. (See the Critics' Note on pages 78–79 for a description of these categories.) The investigator did not indicate the procedure he followed to handle the disproportionate frequency-in-categories problem. If an acceptable procedure for controlling the disproportionate number of boys and girls in the two conditions were used, then the comparison between conditions would *not* be misleading.

5b. QUESTION:

"Background data were collected and analyzed for both pupils and teachers." What data were collected and was it important that the investigator analyze them?

5b. ANSWER:

Pupil IQ and reading test scores were available.[2] Information about age, teaching experience, and college degree was obtained from the 11 teachers. Other information concerning both pupils and teachers may have been collected but was not reported.

Yes, it was important that such data were collected and analyzed, especially in the case of the pupils. Since only 11 classes were involved in the study, and thus gross inequalities between groups are possible, it is important to know how these background variables differ for Conditions A and B. Student data are also of value for the purpose of understanding the limits of permissible generalizations. Since the teacher influence was minimal, teacher differences are not so important as pupil differences.

5c. QUESTION:

On page 76, the investigator indicates that his criterion for determining whether a background variable should be used as, ". . . a possible covariant (i.e., covariate) on subsequent analyses of the criterion data . . . ," is whether pupils in the two conditions differ significantly (in a statistical sense) on that variable. Is this a good criterion to use? Why?

5c. ANSWER:

---

[2] Some kind of pretest was mentioned in "Results."

This is a technical question, the answer to which you are not necessarily expected to know. Our answer is, "NO." The criterion which was quoted assumes, incorrectly, that failure to reject the null hypothesis is equivalent to establishing its truth. Merely because the differences in reading scores and IQ scores for students in Condition A and Condition B are not statistically significant does not mean the two groups are identical in these regards. There is sufficient difference between the groups which could go a long way toward explaining the difference on the criterion variable. Further, the investigator failed to recognize another important reason for including a covariate—namely, to increase the precision (power) of the statistical test. Although beyond the scope of this book, suffice it to say that even if the two groups were equal on these background variables, it may still be a good idea to employ them as covariates in order to increase the likelihood of a true difference on the criterion variable being detected.[3]

6. QUESTION:

The construction of the criterion test of achievement is described in "Collection of Data." Reread this section if you need to refresh your memory.

6a. QUESTION:

Do you agree that ". . . only the total achievement score was of concern in this phase of the investigation."? Give reasons for your answer.

6a. ANSWER:

Absolutely not! Although the investigator may expect achievement to be better on all questions for pupils in Condition A, surely he must expect the most dramatic differences to occur on questions tapping higher level skills. When possible, as in this case, it is important to provide data which relate to predictions growing out of one's conceptualization of what is going on. Failure to provide mean and variability measures for both groups

---

[3] For a further discussion of some of the ideas presented in this paragraph, read Kenneth D. Hopkins, *Preventing the Number One Misinterpretation of Behavioral Research or How to Increase Statistical Power*. Laboratory of Educational Research, University of Colorado, Boulder 80302.

on all subtests is a serious weakness of this study. (In a later study the investigator provided such data.)

6b. QUESTION:

From a pool of 59 items, 42 items were selected and 17 were eliminated. On what basis was the decision made to accept an item? On what basis were the 17 items eliminated?

6b. ANSWER:

We are told that there was almost unanimous agreement on the classification of the 42 items actually included in the criterion test. We are not told, however, the reasons for excluding 17 of the original 59 items and we can only assume that at least some of them were eliminated because the judges could not agree on the appropriate level.

6c. QUESTION:

Do you feel that each item measured the level of cognitive ability that was intended? Why?

6c. ANSWER:

We remain skeptical especially that the higher level abilities of synthesis and evaluation were actually measured since it is most difficult to devise multiple-choice questions which truly measure these skills. Further, since the instructional materials were different for the two conditions, it is possible that a single question could be measuring at different cognitive levels for different students because of this differential prior instruction. For example, suppose that a question and answer *used in the instruction* under Condition A concerned the evaluation of a particular content area. A question in the criterion test asking for an evaluation of a similar area would not be as novel a task for students in Condition A. For those students such a question would not be measuring at this "highest" level (evaluation) but rather it would be measuring lower level skills. Just because an item contains the word "evaluate" does not mean that it will necessarily measure a student's evaluative ability. It is indeed unfortunate that no examples of questions from the instructional materials and the criterion test were shown as evidence that the investigators were able to overcome these difficulties.

It is, of course, important that competent judges be used to classify the items. One point made above is that proper classification requires more than competent judges. We believe the items cannot be classified accurately into the categories employed in this study without knowledge of the students' prior instruction.

6d. QUESTION:

How important is it that this classification task be done accurately? Explain.

6d. ANSWER:

Had subtest scores been reported, as we suggested they should be in our answer to 6a, then the correct assignment of item to taxonomy category would have been very important indeed. Since only the total score was reported and the same criterion test was given to both groups, it probably was not important that the six categories be equally represented and some classification mistakes certainly could be tolerated.

6e. QUESTION:

Publishers of tests which are used to make decisions about individuals often consider reliability indices of .90 or more as "high" (i.e., good) and indices of less than .70 as "poor." The investigator seems to be unhappy with a reliability index of .68. Should he be? Why?

6e. ANSWER:

This is a technical question, the answer to which you are not necessarily expected to know. Our answer is NO. A high reliability coefficient is not required for a criterion measure in a research study comparing groups. High reliability assures us that differences in test scores are not due to measurement error. Unless a test has high reliability differences in an individual's test scores (used to measure "gain" or to determine his relative strong areas) may be due to measurement error. In a research study comparing groups, what are being compared are not the differences between two individual scores but rather the differences in means, each based on the scores of many individuals. Although any one score may have measurement error, the "too high" and "too low" errors will balance out over many people, leaving us quite confident that this mean score is fairly free of measurement error.[4] That is why we can tolerate a lower reliability in the measures we use in research studies which deal with the estimation of group averages. The value of .68 reported by the investigator is quite acceptable.

7. QUESTION:

If you need to refresh your memory, reread the section "Experimental Material and Procedure."

7a. QUESTION:

On page 77, the investigator indicated that it was important that the unit to be studied be one about which the subjects did not have ". . . abundant prior knowledge." Do you agree? Give reasons for your answer.

7a. ANSWER:

---

[4] Reliability means consistency of measurement. If a test consistently gives systematic errors, i.e., errors which are consistently too high or consistently too low, then we say the test is invalid, but it may be reliable. Unreliability occurs because of *random* measurement errors, which, if averaged over enough people (or over many test items) will balance out. Means of many scores or very long tests are usually very reliable.

Yes, we feel it was wise for the investigator to select a topic about which the students did not have abundant prior knowledge. Using such a topic insured that the question and answering procedures would have a chance to make a difference because there were still many things the students could learn. In other words, if students already knew a great deal about a topic, leaving little to learn before the study began, then one procedure of instruction could not be expected to result in more learning than another. A second reason is that when students have different levels of prior knowledge about a subject, it is difficult to construct items which will measure at the same cognitive level for all students. (Recall our answer to 6c above.)

Many students who read this study answered YES for a reason different from the ones we gave above. They felt that the students in the study with prior knowledge would have an unfair advantage and another extraneous factor would be introduced. This would certainly be true, but it should not be a cause for concern unless it is suspected that the students in one of the two groups had, on the average, more prior knowledge than the other group.

Other students answered Question 7a NO and remarked that knowledge of some facts is important, for without such knowledge the students in the study could not be expected to analyze and evaluate. This is true; however the issue is *not* whether the students in the study should have this information (they should), but whether they should be given this information *before* they are exposed to the instructional materials.

7b. QUESTION:

Note that 48% of the questions used in Condition A were in the analysis and evaluation categories; in Condition B 87% of the questions were in the knowledge category. Alternatively, the investigator could have had all the questions in Condition A in the analysis and evaluation categories and all the questions in Condition B in the knowledge category. Would this have been an improvement? Why?

7b. ANSWER:

Before giving our answer to Question 7b, note that the *kinds-of-questions-asked* represents, in this study, the variable which is under the control of the investigator—the variable being manipulated. In appraising the work of others, pay particular attention to the levels or conditions which are being used. The results depend upon it.

If it is true that asking higher level questions really makes a difference, then the alternative distribution proposed involving 100% or 0% in a given category, would give the investigator the best chance to discover differences between conditions. As one student put it, to do otherwise would, ". . . water down the effectiveness . . . ," of the experimental treatment.

On the other hand, the ratios of the different kinds of questions the investigator chose to compare are more typical of what one would expect to find in existing materials or in the questioning patterns of teachers. We approve of the investigator's decision to make the balance of question types more closely resemble present and sound practices rather than to use conditions as different as possible. Clearly, use of either distribution is justified.

7c. QUESTION:

Was the readability analysis a wise thing to do? Explain.

7c. ANSWER:

Yes, to conduct a readability analysis was a wise decision, although reporting readability data separately for the two groups would have been preferable. The readability analysis would have been important had the investigator failed to find differences in favor of Condition A. If that had occurred, one explanation for finding no differences, namely that the reading materials were too hard, could be ruled out by the fact that the mean reading level was within the range of fifth and sixth grade pupils. As one person answering Question 7c put it, the readability analysis, ". . . knocked out the possibility of massive inability to comprehend the questions."

Further, if Condition A students had not done better than the other students, we might have wondered if the higher level questions and answers were more difficult to read. The plausibility of this explanation could be assessed by having readability figures shown separately for materials used in Conditions A and B.

Notice that a reading difficulty index was computed for the *answers* as well as for the questions. This alerts us to the fact that the answers are, in all probability, more than cryptic responses and that by providing answers, additional instruction must have been given. The implication of this will be evident in the answer to the next question.

7d.   QUESTION:

Is it possible to compare the content of the questions and answers used in the instruction to the criterion test questions? If not, is this inability a serious shortcoming? Give reasons.

7d.   ANSWER:

No, we are not told how similar the questions asked in the criterion test were to the questions *and answers* given in the instruction. This omission is probably the most serious shortcoming of the study. We know only that *during instruction* different questions and answers were given to the two different groups. It is extremely difficult, if not impossible, to choose criterion test items upon which these differences in the instructional materials had no bearing. That the investigator does not mention this problem and report in detail how it was circumvented is a serious weakness. It suggests that the differences between the two conditions could be accounted for entirely by the different content of the instructional materials rather than by the practice of answering analysis and evaluation questions alone. This possibility is made more likely by the fact that the answers provided for the evaluation and analysis questions were admitted by the investigator to be more complicated than those for the knowledge ones.

8.   QUESTION:

If you need to refresh your memory, reread the section "Analysis of Data," page 77. Do you approve of using sex and reading achievement as additional variables in the analysis? Why?

8. ANSWER:

Yes. Inclusion of these variables helps to determine the generalizability of the findings. Because there was presumably little interaction between these variables and the treatment variable, it means that the differences between the scores under the two conditions seemed to be about the same for both sexes and across the reading groups. If, for example, the higher level questions and answers were relatively less effective with poor readers this would show up as an interaction between treatment and reading achievement. By including reading achievement and sex as variables in the analysis the investigator could assess the limits to the generalizability of the results in these respects.

It was also important to include these two variables because they were explicity mentioned in the statement of the hypothesis of the study (p. 75) and, thus, a complete test of this hypothesis requires their inclusion.

Some students who read the study made a good case in support of inclusion of one of the two variables. A separate analysis by sex was deemed necessary because of the difference in boy/girl ratios in the two treatment conditions. Others argued that the reading variable was very important to include because of the suspected relationship between reading and performance on the criterion task.

9. QUESTION:

Reread, "Results" on page 78, including Table 1. (You may wish to review the Critics' Note regarding the interpretation of Table 1.)

9a. QUESTION:

Note that the investigator refers to pre-achievement scores. Did he ever report how these scores were obtained? Regardless of whether or not he did so, do you think it was a good idea to obtain such scores? Once obtained, should they have been used? Why?

9a. ANSWER:

The nature of the pre-achievement scores was not specified. They could have been previous achievement grades in social studies. They could have been scores on the criterion test administered before the textbook and special materials were used. If the latter is the case, there is a slight danger that seeing the criterion test ahead of time would be of greater help to students in one condition than in the other. The investigator did mention on page 76, however, that the reading and IQ scores were not used as the covariates; that is, they were not used as the pretest.

Once the pre-achievement scores were obtained, it was a good idea to adjust the criterion scores on the basis of differences on the pre-achievement scores not only to equate the groups, but (as mentioned in answer to 5c) to give greater power to the analysis. The investigator should have told us how the two groups differed on these pre-achievement variables or should have described them more clearly.

9b. QUESTION:

Find the number 9.85 in the *F* column of Table 1. Is the difference in mean scores for students in the two treatment groups statistically significant? Does the number 9.85, by itself, indicate which treatment group performed better?

9b. ANSWER:

This *F* number, as indicated by the footnote appearing in Table 1 in the article, signifies that the means for the two treatment groups are significantly different. The *F* test, however, does not indicate which group scored higher but only that the differences could not reasonably be accounted for by chance alone. We have to look at the mean values to find out which group did better. In this report, we must rely on the statement in the text that Condition A pupils performed better.

9c. QUESTION:

Does the investigator ever indicate the numerical value of the differences in mean scores for students in the two treatment conditions? If so, what is it? If not, should he have done so?

9c. ANSWER:

A surprising deficiency is the failure to report the criterion means for the two groups.[5] We do not know if the difference in means is large or small. To find statistical significance in mean differences is only the initial step in a proper interpretation of a research study. If the difference were as much as half a standard deviation the difference would have important implications; if the difference were only 1/100th of a standard deviation, even though the difference was statistically reliable, it would lack practical significance. The magnitude of the differences should definitely have been given.

10. QUESTION:

If you need to refresh your memory, reread the discussion section, pages 78–80. The investigator indicates that this study suggests that questions requiring analysis and evaluation ". . . stimulated individuals to utilize general viewpoints regarding the information embedded in the task"; forced "mental juggling" of the materials; led to greater ". . . interaction with the materials presented," and have the potential, ". . . to make pupils uneasy." What evidence supports these suggestions?

10. ANSWER:

---

[5] Note that the number 10.05 in Table 1 is not the difference in group means. Rather, it is the result of an intermediate calculaion in the analysis of covariance.

None that we know of. It is true that students given the greater proportion of "analysis" and "evaluation" questions and answers performed better on the criterion test. But the study was not designed to determine how this superior performance came about. The statements of the investigator quoted in Question 10 represent admitted guesses on his part of changes occurring *inside* the student rather than assertions based on reported evidence. It is quite acceptable for an investigator to report his speculations as long as they are clearly labeled so that the reader can recognize them as unsupported views.

11. QUESTION:

Assume that the research were redone so as to overcome the criticisms mentioned earlier and that similar findings in favor of Condition A resulted. What limitations would still remain to this *single study* which would prevent one from generalizing with confidence that questions of higher cognitive levels generally stimulate higher achievement?

11. ANSWER:

The study investigates one topic, in one subject area, for students in one grade, from one suburban school system. It is limited to written self-instructional materials. We do not know if the findings would hold up for the situation in which teachers ask the same questions. Further, only achievement immediately after study was measured. Of more importance is the long-term impact as measured by a delayed post-test. A single study cannot have universal applicability. This study did look at both sexes and various reading achievement levels. We do not fault the investigator for not including more topics, delayed post-testing, and so forth. We only mention these "extensions" to alert you to those situations to which the results might not apply.

7

Effects of Positive Social Reinforcement
on Regressed Crawling
of a Nursery School Child[*1]

Florence R. Harris / Margaret K. Johnston
C. Susan Kelley / Montrose M. Wolf

Use of social reinforcement procedures to help a child substitute already established walking behavior for recently reacquired crawling behavior was studied in a nursery school situation. Adult attention was systematically given as an immediate consequence of one behavior and withheld as an immediate consequence of the other behavior. Results indicated that (a) adult attention had powerful reinforcement values; (b) reversal of reinforcement procedures had distinct positive effects; and (c) systematic use of reinforcement principles brought about rapid changes in behavior, seeming to facilitate both child learning and adult teaching.

This paper reports a use of positive social reinforcement procedures to help a nursery school child substitute well-developed walking behavior for recently reacquired crawling behavior. Princi-

ples of reinforcement have long been established through experimental research with infrahuman subjects. Recently, many of these principles have also been demonstrated with human beings and have been successfully applied to practical problems. Examples of the latter include Ferster and DeMyer's (1961) study of autistic children, Brady and Lind's (1961) treatment of functional blindness, and Ayllon and Haughton's (1962) work with psychotic patients. Ferster and Brady applied the principles in a controlled laboratory situation. Ayllon, however, made applications in a "natural" situation, comparable to the setting in the present study.

* *Originally appeared in the* Journal of Educational Psychology, *Volume 55, 1964, pp. 35–41. Copyright 1964 by the American Psychological Association and reproduced by permission.*

[1] The authors gratefully acknowledge indebtedness to S. W. Bijou, D. M. Baer, and J. S. Birnbrauer, without whose counsel and encouragement this study would not have been possible. R. G. Wahler also contributed generously to the development of observation techniques.

Application of reinforcement principles to nursery school children may be an important step in the process of learning more about child behavior and its relation to guidance practices. Such knowledge relates directly not only to teacher guidance at school but also to parent guidance of children in the home.

The main concern of the study was to see *(a)* whether presentation of positive social reinforcement by teachers could be used to help a 3-year-old use her already well-established walking behavior more frequently; *(b)* if this occurred, whether withdrawing such reinforcement weakened the behavior; and *(c)* whether reinstating social reinforcement practices re-established walking behavior. The reason for the second and third objectives was, of course, to attempt to demonstrate that the positive reinforcing stimuli used were, in fact, the determining conditions in such behavior change. Conclusive data were essential to effective guidance of the child at school, as well as to subsequent counseling with the child's parents.

CRITICS' NOTE:

The chronology of this study can be conveniently divided into several periods. During the first two weeks of her nursery school experience, Dee showed strong withdrawal behavior and was off her feet most of the time. During the third and fourth weeks, the teacher reinforced on-feet behavior with the result that "Dee's behavior was indistinguishable from that of the rest of the children." Next came a crucial two-day period in which Dee was given special attention during her *off-feet* behavior (the reversed reinforcement contingencies). The results of this change in reinforcement pattern are shown in Curves 1 and 2 in Figure 1. Thereafter, the regular reinforcement of on-feet behavior was resumed. The results for the first two days after the start of this second reversal of

procedures are shown in Curves 3 and 4 in Figure 1.

METHOD

Subject

The subject was a girl 3.4 years old who had just enrolled in a university nursery school. She will hereafter be referred to as Dee. Dee was the oldest child in her family, having two younger brothers, one 18 months old and one 8 months old. The parents were a pleasant and likeable young couple. Both held college degrees, the father also having an advanced degree. He was well launched upon a professional career. The mother seemed a warm and responsive person whose primary interest was her family.

Dee was one of 12 children in the nursery school group of 6 boys and 6 girls. Ages ranged from 3 years to 3.5 years. Two teachers supervised the group, which attended school mornings for 2.5 hours 5 days a week.

On the first day of school Dee showed unusually strong withdrawal behavior. That is, she crouched on the floor most of the time, turning her head away or hiding her face in her arms whenever an adult or a child approached. She did not attempt to remain close to her mother, who sat in one corner of the room or of the play yard. Dee spoke to no one and crawled from indoors to outdoors and from place to place as school activities shifted.

Dee continued to show little reaction to her mother's presence during subsequent days at school. On the seventh day of school her mother was leaving a few minutes after bringing her and coming back to get her 2 hours later (the same as most of the other mothers), with Dee seemingly indifferent to her presence or absence.

Typically, Dee removed and put on her wraps while sitting on the floor in the locker area, and then either left them on the floor or crawled to her locker and stuffed them in. Sometimes she pulled herself to her feet with her hands on the locker edges and hung her wraps on the appropriate hooks. Then, dropping to hands and knees, she crawled to an out-of-the-way spot and sat or crouched. She crawled into the bathroom beside other children before snack time and occasionally pulled herself to a standing position beside a sink to rinse her hands. She did not use a toilet at school, but remained dry. From the sink she usually crawled to a group gathered for snacks and sat near a teacher and some children. She usually accepted and ate a snack, but remained impassive, somber, and silent. The rest of the group talked, laughed, and in general responded freely to both the teachers and to other children. The usual teacher approaches to Dee (friendly, warm, and solicitous) resulted in strong withdrawal behavior as described.

Her mother reported that the same behavior was strongly evident when visitors came to her home or when Dee was taken on visits. Otherwise Dee was described as "gentle, sweet, and cooperative." The mother was, or course, greatly concerned over her child's withdrawal behavior. It was this concern which had, at least in part, prompted her to enroll Dee in a nursery school.

By the end of the second week of school Dee was avoiding all contacts with children or adults and avoiding the use of most material and equipment. A half-hour record written at this time showed Dee in a standing position for only 6.7% of the time, once at her locker and once at a bathroom sink. For 93.3% of the observation period she sat or crouched on hands and knees. She had spoken only a few words during these weeks. She had spoken only to teachers. The words had consisted of a soft "no" or "yes" at snack time. In staff discussion, teachers gave a conservative estimate that at least 75% of her time at school, exclusive of group times when everyone was normally seated, Dee was in off-feet positions. Since this behavior

prevented her participation in the broad range of available learning activities, and since the behavior was such as to be readily observable by students and by staff, the staff decided to help the child by applying reinforcement principles.

Initial Reinforcement Procedures

It was decided that the teachers should attempt to weaken Dee's off-feet behavior by withholding attention (giving neutral stimulation) when Dee was off her feet. An exception to this might occur at group times, when attention was to be a minimum consonant with courtesy. The withdrawal-of-attention procedure was to be casually implemented by a teacher simply by becoming fully occupied with any one of the many immediate requirements always confronting nursery school teachers. In other words, teacher attention was to show no obvious relationship to Dee's off-feet behavior. Teachers were also to avoid displaying any behavior that might suggest anger, disappointment, disgust, shame, or dislike. There was to be nothing punitive about their behavior.

Concurrent with the above procedure, on-feet behavior was to be immediately positively reinforced. That is, Dee was to be given attention whenever she displayed standing behavior. Since she stood up so infrequently, and so briefly, the behaviors closely approximating standing were also to be reinforced during initial days. That is, when she rose even partially to her feet, as well as when she stood, a teacher was to give her attention. Such attention was to consist of going immediately to her and making appropriate interested comments about what she was doing. Sample comments might be, "You hung that up all by yourself. You know just where it goes," and "It's fun to let water slide over your fingers. It feels nice and warm, doesn't it?" A teacher's attention behavior was to convey to Dee that she was liked, appreciated, and considered capable.

In order for a reinforcer to be most effective, it must immediately follow the behavior to be changed. Therefore, to ensure that Dee received immediate positive reinforcement for standing positions, one teacher was assigned to remain within range of her at all times, carrying major responsibility for this aspect of the guidance program. The other teacher was to carry major responsibility for the program of the rest of the children in the group. The teacher assigned the role of giving positive reinforcement every time Dee got on her feet was selected because she seemed to have a good relationship with the child. For example, Dee usually crawled to her group at snack time.

Recording Behavior Changes

No special plans beyond teacher observations were made, at first, for recording behavior changes and the incidence of reinforcement. A staff member recorded the previously mentioned half-hour observation. Teachers, of course, observed Dee's behavior from the first day and recorded the kinds of incident notes that they took on behavior of each child in the group. Teachers' subjective estimates based on their daily observations were also used. In addition, subjective estimates by students in an observation course were considered. These students first observed Dee's group during the second week of school. All noted her behavior at once, although no reference had been made to it in class, and discussed it at the next class meeting.

Two weeks after reinforcement procedures were begun, several students volunteered to procure more adequate recordings of Dee's behavior for purposes of making a more systematic study and to satisfy their own interest. Most of the data presented in Figure 1, Curves 2 and 3, were secured by these students, each recording for an hour. Their efforts could provide only about

4 hours of data. The remainder (about 2.5 hours) were recorded by a staff member.

RESULTS OF INITIAL PROCEDURES

The intensive recording of Dee's behavior by students and staff was stimulated by dramatic results of application of the planned procedures. Within 1 week from the start of reinforcing on-feet positions and ignoring off-feet behavior, Dee was on her feet a large proportion of time. Percentages of time on feet and time off feet seemed to have reversed. By the end of 2 weeks (1 month after she entered school) Dee's behavior was indistinguishable from that of the rest of the children. She talked readily, often with smiling animation, to the teacher administering the planned schedule of social reinforcement. She used all of the outdoor equipment with vigor and enthusiasm. She worked with obvious enjoyment at the easels, with housekeeping-play facilities, and with such materials as clay.

However, Dee was not making direct responses to children, although she engaged in much parallel activity; nor did she initiate contacts with children or with the other teacher, ignoring them for the most part. But she accepted without position changes any approach or suggestion made by the other teacher or a staff member, and on the whole made use of available learning experiences as effectively as most of the other children in the group. She could no longer be considered severely withdrawn at school. Her mother also reported a remarkable improvement in her social behavior at home.

REVERSING REINFORCEMENT PROCEDURES

In order to be sure that the reinforcement procedures applied had been the significant causative factor in Dee's change in behavior, the teaching staff was obliged to pursue the study through two more processes: *(a)* reinstate off-feet behavior, and then *(b)* once again establish appropriate on-feet behaviors. In addition to personal reluctance to institute these processes, the staff at this point seriously questioned their ability to succeed in getting Dee again into off-feet behavior. She appeared to be getting strong reinforcement from her vigorous and exploratory activities, from exchange of speech with adults, and from parallel activities with children. It seemed unlikely that manipulation of adult social reinforcers could now have an effect strong enough to compete with these newly experienced reinforcements. Partly because of this doubt and partly because of the necessity to be certain that adult social reinforcement had been the critical independent variable, the staff agreed to attempt to reinstate Dee's off-feet behavior.

The teachers' procedure in extinguishing on-feet behavior was to reverse their previous reinforcement contingencies: that is *(a)* to give no attention when Dee was on feet, and *(b)* give continuous attention when she was off feet. The staff agreed that any evidence of detrimental effects, such as loss of speech, crying, or other emotional behavior, would be sufficient cause for terminating the plan.

At this phase of the study students assisted in getting more detailed and extensive records.

RESULTS OF REVERSE PROCEDURES

During the first morning of giving Dee attention (reinforcement) during off-feet but not during on-feet behavior, a 2-hour record was kept. Each 30-second period of these 2 hours was then arbitrarily considered as a discrete unit of behavior. Units of time off feet

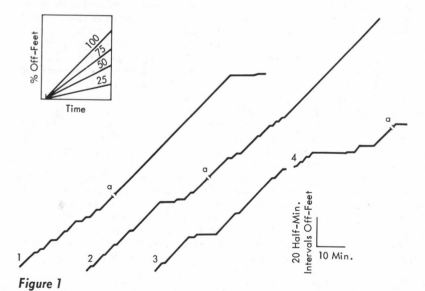

Figure 1

Subject's off-feet behavior on four different mornings: the first (Curve 1) and second (Curve 2) mornings of giving attention during off-feet and ignoring on-feet behavior, and the third (Curve 3) and fourth (Curve 4) mornings of giving attention during on-feet and ignoring off-feet behavior. Breaks at Points (a) indicate snack times averaging 12 minutes duration, which were not included in the data.

were then plotted in a cumulative graph, the horizontal axis showing time and the vertical axis showing number of off-feet units (see Figure 1, Curve 1). Rises on the graph indicate periods of time off feet, while plateaus indicate periods on feet. Exclusive of a group time of 12 minutes, during which children were expected to be seated together, Dee spent 75.7% of the morning off her feet. On the following day, which was similarly recorded and graphed, she spent 81.9% of the morning off her feet (see Figure 1, Curve 2). There were no signs on either day of detrimental effects on Dee other than those associated with behaving from a crawling position.

CRITICS' NOTE:

Figure 1 is a bit difficult to interpret. The length of the line in the horizontal direction indicates the length of time Dee was being systematically observed. Thus, the longest observation period was during the second day in which attention procedures were reversed; the shortest for the two days immediately following. The steepness of the curve to the horizontal axis indicates the degree to which Dee was *off* her feet. Thus, Dee was *on* her feet the greatest length of time for the last day shown because Curve 4 is not very steep. On the critical first day in which reverse procedures were followed (Curve 1) Dee was off her feet most of the time except toward the end of the observation period when, as shown by the bend in the curve to the horizontal position, she was on her feet. Do not be misled by the fact that Curve 4 is "in the air." The positioning of the curves was arbitrary. We suspect that Curve 4 was placed alongside Curve 3 in order to save space, or to remind the reader that the last two curves refer to consecutive days under the same reinforcement condition.

With nearly 82% of her time

spent off her feet, clearly Dee had returned to her old behavior pattern. The staff therefore decided at that point to reinstate on-feet behavior.

SECOND REVERSAL OF PROCEDURES

Reinforcement procedures were again reversed; that is, teachers gave steady attention whenever Dee got to her feet and gave no attention when she was off her feet. Figure 1, Curve 3, graphs her off-feet behavior for the first hour of the third subsequent day. During the observation, Dee spent 75.9% of the time off her feet and only 24.1% on feet. Teachers reported, however, that during the last half of the morning, for which a written record was not secured, Dee spent most of the time in vigorous activity on her feet. Figure 1, Curve 4, graphs the first hour of the following day. Dee spent 37.8% of the hour off feet and 62.2% on feet. Again, the second hour she was reported to have spent on her feet almost steadily. From this day on, Dee's behavior was in every way adequate and she seemed happily occupied.

DISCUSSION

The data strongly indicate that adult attention changed Dee's behavior in the desired direction (was the significant independent variable), and that for Dee adults were very powerful reinforcers. It also seems that social reinforcement principles, carefully delineated and applied, can provide effective and efficient guidance tools for teachers and parents of young children.

Although the graphs show only the time Dee spent in the positional behaviors being specifically controlled, other interesting behavioral changes occurred during the study. These changes seemed to be largely salutory and to develop with unusual rapidity. Some changes seemed causally linked to the fact that reinforcement contingencies were reversed twice, a possibility that merits further study.

Much of the normal behavior, in addition to positional changes, resulted from the initial process of reinforcing only on-feet behaviors. This normal behavior included *(a)* ready verbalization with one adult (the assistant teacher), *(b)* adequate verbalization in response to questions from other adults but little if any initiation of contacts with them, *(c)* parallel activities with other children but little if any verbalization to them, and *(d)* play using a wide range of materials and equipment. These changes occurred within 2 weeks of instituting the reinforcement procedures.

When a shift was made from reinforcement of on-feet to reinforcement of off-feet behavior some loss was observed, but significant gains appeared as well. The major loss appeared to be in vigorous motor activities such as jumping and running. This, of course, was a direct result of Dee's off-feet positions. Another change that appeared to involve both loss and gain came in Dee's adult relationships. On the first day on which testing procedures began (reinforcing off-feet behavior and giving no reinforcement while on feet), Dee tended to move away from the reinforcing teacher and for the first time to accept, even seek, attention from the other teacher. Reinforcement from both the teachers maintained off-feet behavior during much of the morning. During the first part of the morning, Dee made many short trials of standing positions. After 35 minutes of this alternating up and down behavior, Dee remained off her feet until close to the end of the morning. During this time she spoke readily to the second teacher, asking questions, asking for help occasionally, and answering the teacher's comments and questions. She also engaged in play with materials, near other children. Occasionally she exchanged words with the latter, a new aspect of

behavior for Dee. Part of her activity consisted of going upright on her knees from one play situation to another. At the doll-corner table where two other children were making cookies with dough and utensils, Dee insisted on staying on her knees beside the table although the teacher pointed out that there was an empty chair beside her and that the other children were seated. Dee's response was, "I *want* to be on the floor doing it."

Near the close of that morning (reinforcement of off-feet positions) Dee went outdoors again. She got to her feet at the door, ran across the yard to where another child played on packing boxes and boards, and joined the other in vigorous running and jumping. This play was at a distance from both teachers, and of course neither teacher approached. The play continued with much laughter, shouts, and some talking. It drew two more children. Dee's mother arrived shortly. She showed great pleasure in finding Dee in joyous active play with other children. She stood near, smiling and commending Dee's and her friends' balancing and jumping stunts. Dee was smiling, eyes sparkling, when she and her mother left. Dee waved from the gate and called "Goodbye!" to both the teachers. Hence, it seems apparent that there were sources of social reinforcement not in coordination with those controlled in the experiment.

Teachers and the observer judged that the first day of reinstating (reinforcing) off-feet positions *(a)* precipitated much off-feet behavior; *(b)* had little or no effect on the amount and quality of Dee's verbalizations; *(c)* had surprisingly slight effect on the amount, diversity, and quality of Dee's use of materials and equipment; *(d)* may have extended Dee's social experiences to include satisfying contacts with the other teacher; *(e)* had reduced considerably Dee's approaches to the reinforcing teacher; and *(f)* may have encouraged her to initiate play with other children, play that seemed positively reinforcing to all the children involved. In other words, the positive effects of reversing reinforcement contingencies seemed to outweigh by far the momentary negative results.

During the second day of reinforcement of off-feet behavior, the first two thirds of the session was punctuated by tentative bursts of standing. During two of the longer bursts, Dee moved about the yard pushing over the movable upright equipment. Teachers presented no reinforcement. Periods of standing dwindled to steady off-feet behavior. Even the arrival of Dee's mother at the end of the morning did not draw Dee to her feet. Mother walked across to her and somewhat impatiently pulled her to her feet and took her away. Although Dee seemed to lose only those vigorous behaviors for which standing postures were essential, the investigators judged that her behavior for the 2 days gave sufficient demonstration of the power of adult social reinforcement in changing her behavior. Rather than risk possible loss in the areas of verbal or child-child social behavior, they decided to terminate the study by again reinforcing on-feet behavior. In addition, they decided to reinforce all verbal behavior, regardless of Dee's position. Another influential aspect in terminating the "test" procedure was that it was distasteful to the investigators and therefore made them apprehensive about its effects on Dee. Further, no observer besides the teachers could be available during the following 2 days of school.

During approximately 1 hour of the third day of again reinforcing on-feet behavior, plus positive reinforcement of all verbal behavior, a record was taken during the first half of the morning. Teachers reported that during most of the latter half of the morning Dee played vigorously on her feet on climbing equipment with other children, with apparent pleasure and with much reinforcement from adults and

children. The behavior of pushing over equipment, which was at no time followed by presentation of either positive or negative reinforcement, had dropped out entirely. On the fourth day of reinstating on-feet behavior, Dee spent better than 60% of the recorded hour on her feet, a proportion of time which made her positional behavior indistinguishable from that of the group. Teachers noted that some of her standing behavior at this time was sufficiently different from the group mode to be classed as "stunting on equipment." She stood up to swing and also to propel the long rocking-board, two activities usually pursued by the threes in a sitting position. The latter part of the morning, Dee played vigorously with children, usually on her feet.

By the end of a week of reinforcing on-feet positions, Dee showed positional behavior that was normal in the group. In addition, she was readily initiating and accepting social contacts with all of the adult staff as well as with several of the children in the group. Within a 5-week period of school attendance, Dee's behavior showed a degree of progress that would have been expected within not less than 5 or 6 months under previous guidance techniques. Her parents were as pleased as the staff over her progress, as well as over their fresh understandings of their roles in helping her develop appropriate social behaviors.

Postchecks made at irregular intervals for a year subsequent to the study showed an average of 35% of school mornings spent in off-feet behavior, all of which was appropriate to the social and individual activities pursued, i.e., crayoning, clay work, dolls. Teachers agree that Dee's improved behavior was stable.

REFERENCES

AYLLON, T., & HAUGHTON, E. Control of the behavior of schizophrenic patients by food. *J. exp. Anal. Behav.*, 1962, 5, 343–352.

BRADY, J. P., & LIND, D. L. Experimental analysis of hysterical blindness. *Arch. gen. Psychiat.*, 1961, 4, 331–339.

FERSTER, C. B., & DeMYER, MARIAN K. The development of performance in autistic children in an automatically controlled environment. *J. chron. Dis.*, 1961, 13, 312–345.

CRITIQUE

1. QUESTION:

Puzzling behaviors occurred during the reversed reinforcement period where *off-feet* behavior was reinforced. Describe these unexpected phenomena.

1. ANSWER:

Dee became *more* socially adjusted during the period when attention was given to off-feet behavior. It was not expected that Dee's return to her off-feet behavior would be accompanied by greater social adjustment. She began, ". . . for the first time to accept, even seek, attention from the other teacher [p. 104]." She also exchanged a few words with the other children, something entirely new for Dee. "The positive effects of reversing reinforcement contingencies seemed to outweigh by far the momentary negative results [p. 105]."

We were also puzzled by another event which was not commented upon by the authors. We would not have expected Dee to return to her predominantly off-feet behavior as quickly as she did on the first day that the reverse reinforcement procedures were instituted. As indicated by the steepness of Curve 1 at its lower left portion, on that first day Dee appears to have been off her feet from the moment she entered nursery school.

2. QUESTION:

The authors conclude that the increased ratio of Dee's on-feet to off-feet behavior was caused by the teacher's positive social reinforcement of the on-feet behavior. Other explanations are possible. Dee's increased on-feet behavior might be explained by at least some of the following: (a) the reinforcement of walking itself; (b) increased familiarity with the nursery setting; (c) the expanded range of rewarding objects (toys and people) made possible by walking; (d) possible physical factors (such as illness, fatigue, physiological maturation). Decide which explanation, *if any,* you think is correct. Give reasons for your choice.

2. ANSWER:

At least some of the factors mentioned in Question 2 would be reasonable explanations for the increased on-feet behavior were it not for the fact that the investigators could change the on-feet to off-feet ratios merely by changing the focus of the teacher's reinforcement. The factors suggested in the four options provided in Question 2 were present during the off-feet reversal time. We are thus led to conclude that the return to high off-feet behavior is most likely due to one factor that was correspondingly changed —the teacher reinforcement procedure. If the teacher's social reinforcement were not a causal factor, removing this reinforcement would not change Dee's on-feet to off-feet behavior ratio.

If you answered that one of the four factors could account for Dee's increased on-feet behavior, you are in a predicament. If any of these factors were responsible for the increased on-feet behavior, then Dee should have continued her improvement during the reversal procedure because these factors were all present at that time. The fact that Dee reverted to her off-feet behavior implies that any effects of these factors were overshadowed by the teacher's positive social reinforcement.

Whether researcher or critic, be alert in any research for other explanations of the results and assess their plausibility. The investigators' use of a manipulated variable design was effective in dealing with what otherwise would have been reasonable alternative explanations.

3. QUESTION:

This study is a cause-and-effect study: attention to on-feet behavior (X) causes a child to change her behavior (Y). It is commonly thought that phenomena are explained when causes can be correctly identified. How can we best explain Dee's behavior? Three forms of explanation are as follows:

A. *The covering law form.* A single instance is explained when it is subsumed under a general law which "covers" the particular case. For example, the specific instance in which a thermometer registers a higher reading when the temperature increases is explained by the general law that heat causes liquid to expand.

B. *The manipulated variable form.* Event X is said to be a cause of Y because when the experimenter permits X to be present, he gets Y, and when he removes X, he fails to get Y.

C. *The coherent pattern form.* Event X is said to relate to event Y when the many descriptive elements in these events are shown to "fit" together to form a pattern of relations. In such a case, multiple causes, some occurring together and some occurring as a sequence of events, are described. Thus, to explain the causal relations between X and Y it is necessary to give a full account of the elements involved. This is the historian's, or case study, form of explanation.

One reason we found this study to be particularly interesting is that the investigators provide a rich assortment of evidence to support the claim that attention to on-feet behavior caused Dee to change her behavior. It is possible to (and we would like you to) explain Dee's behavior using each of the three forms of explanation described above. Specifically, in regard to *each* of these three forms of explanation:

1. cite material from the article itself which could be used to explain the change in Dee's behavior; and

2. give reasons for being critical of each of these explanations.

Thus, for example, your answer to Question 3A (1) would need to identify a general law and show how one could claim it "covers" this particular case. In 3A (2) your response will be a criticism of the explanation presented in 3A (1).

Note: We are *not* asking you to pick one form of explanation as "correct." Critically discuss how each applies in this study.

3. ANSWER:

A. *Covering Law Form*

1) Evidence:

2) Criticism:

B. The Manipulated Variable Form

1) Evidence:

2) Criticism:

C. The Coherent Pattern Form

1) Evidence:

2) Criticism:

3. ANSWER:

A. Covering Law Form

1) Evidence:
   One way to express the covering general law is: behavior is strengthened when it is followed by a reward (reinforcement); conversely, behavior is weakened or eliminated when it is not rewarded. The on-feet behavior was strengthened because it was followed by a reinforcement (adult attention). Animal trainers, teachers, and parents have used something like behavior modification for centuries by providing food, gold stars, or treats when their charges performed desired behaviors. We generally conclude that the cause of behavior change is reward. Dee's change in behavior (from

off-feet to on-feet) is the special case subsumed under the law of reinforcement.

2) Criticism:

The specific instance (the Dee case) in this study does not fit the general law completely. Recall in connection with Question 1 that some of the positive behavior (e.g., greater social adjustment, playing near other children) was NOT weakened when Dee's on-feet behavior was no longer rewarded. It is perfectly acceptable to claim, as the investigators do, ". . . that there were sources of social reinforcement not in coordination with those controlled in the experiment [p. 104]." It is important, however, to be able to identify these reinforcers independently of whether or not they have an effect. If only those actions which change behavior are called reinforcers, then the law that reinforcement changes behavior must be true by definition; it is untestable.

Because it is convenient to do so and not because it is a direct answer to question 3A 2, we make the following two observations about laws and the covering law form of explanation. First, more than one law can account for the same observation. The covering law form thus permits multiple explanations of the same observations. Second, when causal explanations take this covering law form we generally do not ask for further explanation since these events are common and familiar in the experience of most people. But we may find a law-like relation between events X and Y and still feel that the relation has not been adequately explained. For example, we may see that heat causes a liquid substance to expand, but we may still feel that we do not have a completely satisfactory explanation of expansion of liquids. Similarly, we may feel that "reinforcement" is not a satisfactory explanation.

B.   The Manipulated Variable Form

1) Evidence:

Clearly, the investigators were manipulating an event and studying the resulting effects. The investigators purposefully increased teacher attention to Dee's on-feet behavior and gave no attention to off-feet behavior (X present), then purposefully reversed attention procedures (X withdrawn), and finally reinstated the original attention procedure (X again present). Increased on-feet behavior (Y) was evidenced when attention was directed toward it (X present) and when such attention was reversed, (X withdrawn), the investigators failed to get (Y).

2) Criticism:

The manipulated variable form of explanation is usually attacked on grounds that other factors vary as X is manipulated, or that event X is too broadly stated and that the real cause of Y is only some component of event X.

Some students have correctly observed that reinforcement was not withdrawn but rather the particular behavior reinforced was varied. Since Dee received teacher attention all the time, it is not too surprising that some of Dee's changes (e.g., greater social adjustment) did not deteriorate during the two-day reverse reinforcement period. Nevertheless, the conclusion that the specific focus of the reinforcement caused the change in Dee's on-feet to off-feet ratio is not weakened by the reasoning above and this conclusion would seem inescapable if it were not for some added reservations spelled out below.

We are struck by the puzzling fact that Dee resumed her old off-feet habits immediately upon beginning the first day of the two-day period in which attention procedures were reversed. If these attention procedures were such powerful conditioners, then why, on the day immediately following the final reversal of procedures, was there virtually no lessening of off-feet behavior (see Curve 3)?

We are left wondering how much off-feet behavior would have occurred during the critical two-day period had no change in procedure been instituted. The data in Curves 1 and 2 would have been more convincing had similar data been shown for the other children. We are told, for example, that Dee's playmates in the doll corner were also off their feet. The proportion of time a child will spend on his feet depends to some extent upon the type of activity in which he is engaged. We speculate that during these particular two days Dee perhaps chose to spend more time indoors involved in activities that naturally lent themselves to off-feet behavior.

C. The Coherent Pattern Form

1) Evidence:

A case study admits complex events taking place over a significant period of time with many variables. The investigators report many of these descriptive details: the family background; Dee's entry behavior; the puzzling fact that she regressed to crawling (strong withdrawal behavior to usual friendly, warm teacher approaches); mother's reports; the development of the study through the various reinforcement procedures; social adjustment; and post-checks made at irregular intervals for a year subsequent to the study. (Teachers agreed that Dee's improved behavior was stable.) The investigators attempt to show how all these facts fit together in a sensible way.

2) Criticism:

The main criticism is that not enough of Dee's life prior to entry into nursery school is given; nor do we know enough about Dee's life outside nursery school (21 hours of each day). Specifically, we have no information about why Dee might have started to regress to crawling behavior. We could speculate that her younger brothers (aged 8 months and 18 months) were both still crawling and that while they were rewarded (attention given) Dee was not. Finally, we need more description of what other adult and child behavior might have been reinforcing to Dee.

We believe that events are explained when a sufficiently rich description of these events leaves us without further significant questions to ask. The incompleteness of this report leads us to describe it as a demonstration study rather than a case study. It is a demonstration of the application of the principle of reinforcement rather than an explanation of how and why these principles work.

4. QUESTION:

One person wrote that ". . . the study would have been better if: (a) reliability checks had been made on all the recordings; (b) recordings had been available for more time; and (c) there had been better documentation of what was happening at the various times the child was on-feet and off-feet." Do you agree? If not, why not? If yes, do you think such improved record-keeping might have changed the authors' conclusions? In what ways?

4. ANSWER:

We agree. The procedures used in this study were much more casual than those we would generally expect to find in educational and psychological research. Dee was observed systematically only a portion of the time. The change in percent of time off-feet from the two-day reverse reinforcement period to the second reversal period might be accounted for by normal, expected variation. Without a longer, more detailed accounting of percent off-feet statistics, we have little basis for assessing the fluctuation which did occur.

We have no indication of how reliably the observers were able to record Dee's behavior. Particularly welcome would be information on inter-rater reliability, that is, the extent to which the ratings of several judges observing the same occurrences agree. Further, the investigators rely on teachers' judgments and impressions which may be subject to bias due to their own expectancies.

If we had more precise and complete data, the speculations we made in our answer to Question 3B 2 would not have been necessary. Although we doubt that such data would change the main conclusion, there nevertheless remains the possibility that such alternative explanations (chance fluctuation, nature of the activities Dee engaged in, etc.) would be supported.

5. QUESTION:

Cite four or more strengths (i.e., desirable features) of this investigation. Attempt to identify distinct types of strength.

5. ANSWER:

There are many positive things to be said about this investigation. A few strengths are listed below.

1. An experimental situation was manipulated by the investigators. When the independent variable is manipulated by the experimenter, we have a very strong technique for investigating the existence of causal relations. The fact that the investigators provided, then removed, and then restored attention to the on-feet behavior of Dee provides strong evidence that this attention was a cause of whatever effects varied systematically with changes in attention. The evidence is much stronger than, for example, if the investigators merely increased attention to the on-feet behavior and observed the results.

2. The investigators displayed a concern for the possible negative consequences on Dee of their study. The investigators were prepared to terminate the reversal condition if Dee showed, ". . . any evidence of detrimental effects, such as loss of speech, crying, or other emotional behavior." Researchers do not have unlimited rights to manipulate their subjects. The rationale that society will benefit from such findings is not sufficient to harm, psychologically or physically, the particular subjects used in search of greater knowledge. The researcher has an obligation to protect the individual.

3. We commend the investigators for seizing an interesting opportunity (the discovery of Dee) for special study. Significant research is often conducted when the research is triggered by a puzzling observation or fortuitous event. Had the investigators first planned a careful system of observation, for example, and then sought to find a Dee, a more smoothly executed study might have been the result, but only if a Dee could then be found. It is better to do what you can with an interesting situation that presents itself than to let it pass unstudied.

4. The study has direct relevance for educational practices. The major variable is one that can be manipulated by teachers in classrooms or other situations. It is in the power of teachers to reinforce desired behaviors by such social

rewards, although we admit that, in some senses, the situation described in this investigation was well suited for this purpose. That the study was conducted in a schooling situation using techniques easily learned facilitates its adoption by others.

5. The study did provide evidence about the effect of positive reinforcement. Thus, in the conduct of the study, supportable knowledge claims were made.

6. One person commented that a strength of the study was:

> To make nursery school teachers and student observers more sensitive about the effectiveness of their own behavior in shaping children's responses. One child changed; many teachers were. One can imagine the hours of meeting time that were devoted to planning and discussing this study and its implication; no doubt this was excellent in-service education of the teachers and their apprentices.

We note the values of research are not limited to the supportable knowledge claims. Inquiry is a form of learning and is often as valuable as a process itself as for the direct results it supports.

7. The investigators considered several dependent variables (e.g., social adjustment) and not just the single variable of on-feet behavior. They were concerned both with the long-range results of the experiment (as evidenced by their follow-up checks) and with the unintended as well as the anticipated outcomes.

8. One child was benefited directly.

9. The problem was well stated, the article was logically organized, and the nature of the reinforcement was explicitly defined.

8

Motivation and Creativity: The Context Effect*

David Elkind / Joann Deblinger
David Adler[1]

Thirty-two children were tested on three creativity measures. Each child was tested twice, once when taken from an ongoing "interesting" task and once when taken from an ongoing "uninteresting" task. When the children expected to return to an "uninteresting" task they were almost twice as "creative" as they were when they anticipated the resumption of an "interesting" activity.

The present study was suggested by some unexpected findings that we encountered in our evaluation of the innovative educational program of the World of Inquiry School (WOIS) in Rochester, New York. This school offers a non-graded flexible curriculum for a pupil population selected to provide a representative sample of the racial, ethnic, and socioeconomic distribution of the community at large. Among the most innovative features of the school is the availability of a number of "interest areas" where children can elect to spend their afternoons in science, shop, art, music, or other activities. Both teachers and pupils find it a highly engaging setting in which to live, work, and learn.

As part of the evaluation of this program, we examined not only children at the WOIS but also a control group attending public schools in various parts of the city. The control children were selected from names on the waiting list for acceptance into the WOIS and were matched with their WOIS counterparts for age, sex, race, socioeconomic status, and educational

* *Originally appeared in the* American Educational Research Journal, *May 1970, pp. 351–357. Reprinted with permission of the American Educational Research Association and the senior author.*

[1] We are grateful to William C. Young, Director of Project Unique, Bill Pugh, principal of the World of Inquiry School, and to the teachers and pupils for their friendly cooperation.

achievement. Among the non-academic measures employed as part of the evaluation battery were three "creativity" tests (the class concept, similarities, and alternate uses tests) that had been used by other investigators (Kogan & Wallach, 1965) and which were reported to have defined a dimension different from test intelligence. It is not our intention here to deal with the issue of whether these tests measure "creativity" or something else. In this regard we tend to side with Cronbach (1968) who argues that "creativity" is too value laden and that names for particular tests should instead be used to designate the measures in question. All we mean to say here is that these tests have been called "creativity" tests in the literature and are currently in widespread use in educational evaluation.

We expected, of course, that children from the WOIS would do better on the "creativity" measures than their matched controls in the public schools. This expectation was based on the assumption that the stimulating environment of the WOIS would encourage greater "creativity" than would the more traditional classroom atmosphere. To our surprise, however, we found that just the opposite of our assumption obtained. In almost every case, the control children in the public schools scored higher on the creativity measures than did the youngsters at the WOIS. It was observed, however, that during the testing many of the public school children appeared reluctant to return to their classroom and seemed to enjoy the testing as a novel and interesting experience. Just the reverse appeared to be true for the WOIS youngsters who had seemed engrossed in what they were doing and hence reluctant to leave for the testing and eager to return to the classroom.

The "creativity" measures that were employed seemed, on the surface at least, to be particularly susceptible to the sort of motivational influence suggested by these observations. All three tests (class concept, similarities and al-

ternate uses) were what might be called "production" tasks in the sense that they required the child to give as many responses as he could to particular materials. The "Alternate Uses Test" to illustrate, requires the subject to "tell me all the different ways in which you can use a newspaper." Likewise, on the Similarities Test, the child is required to say, for one item, "tell me all the ways in which a potato and a carrot are alike." On such tests both the total number of responses and the number of unique responses (a unique response is defined as one not given by the other children) were scored. It seemed reasonable, in view of these considerations, to test the effects of motivation on putative creativity measures in a more rigorous experiment. This was the major aim of the study reported here.

METHOD

Subjects

The subjects were 32 children attending the World of Inquiry School. Four boys and 4 girls were randomly chosen from the 5–6, 7–8, 9–10 and 11–12 age groups present in the school. Twenty-one of the children were white, 10 were black and one was Puerto Rican. This distribution was roughly comparable to the proportions of each group in the larger community. Inasmuch as each child who participated in the study served as his own control, we made no attempt to control for or to equate individual differences in ability. We felt that if the results held for children of different ability and age levels and from different ethnic and socioeconomic backgrounds, they would have greater generality than if a more homogeneous sample participated in the study.

Procedure

Three tests (the class concept, similarities and alternate uses tests) from the Kogan and Wallach (1965) creativity battery were employed. The tests were divided into two parts—on an odd/even item basis–to provide alternate but equivalent forms of the creativity measures. That the forms were indeed equivalent was shown by the fact that we found no significant difference between the total number of responses or between the number of unique responses given to the two forms. Each child took one form of the test when this involved interrupting an ongoing "interesting" activity and the other form when this involved interrupting an ongoing "uninteresting" activity.

The "interesting" condition was determined by the child's own interests as indicated by the teacher. Such activities included playing games, drama, science, reading, art, gym, music, shop and social studies. The child under the "interesting" condition was taken for testing while he engaged in one of his favorite activities. He was told, "Would you please come with me, I have a few games I would like to play with you. After we finish, you can complete whatever you are doing or are working on now." That the ongoing activity was indeed interesting to the child was evidenced by the groans, grimaces and foot dragging that accompanied the examiner's request.

The "uninteresting" activities were constructed by us. Two sheets, one containing 400 letter combinations and another containing 400 number combinations (pairs and triads) were employed. The content and ordering of the letter and number combinations were arrived at by reference to a table of random numbers. The uninteresting tests required the child to circle all of the n's or 6's on the page and were administered in the classroom where the child was told, "Would you please do this reading (math) study skill and when you finish do this math (reading) skill. Read the directions carefully (the directions were then read out loud by the experimenter) and work carefully. Any questions as to what you are to do?"

After the child completed the first "uninteresting" task (about ten to fifteen minutes) he was given the same instructions about leaving to "play games" and about returning to the ongoing activity as he had received under the "interesting" condition. Again, behavioral evidence supported the view that these tasks were indeed uninteresting. The children complained while doing the task, some called it "stupid," and with few exceptions the children were uniformly delighted when their participation in the games was requested.

Half of the children were tested under the "uninteresting" condition first and the "interesting" condition second whereas the reverse held true for the other 16 children. The order in which the two forms of the test were presented was counterbalanced as well. To complete the experimental design, equal numbers of boys and girls at each age level were represented in the two orders of motivating condition and test administration.

Design

The experiment lent itself to a three way analysis of variance design with motivating-condition and order-of-motivating-condition as the within subjects variables and groups-under-order-of-motivating-condition as the between subjects variable. The age variable was not incorporated into the design because of the small number of subjects at each age level, because we did not attempt to equate for ability across age levels and because we had no theoretical basis for predicting a significant age or age by motivational condition interaction effect. A descriptive analysis of the age effects will, however, be presented in the results section.

CRITICS' NOTE:

Replace the first sentence under the subheading "Design" with the following:

The experiment lent itself to an analysis of variance design with motivating-condition as the within subjects variable and order-of-motivating condition and students within order-of-motivating condition as the between subjects variables.

The preceding sentence, which replaces the inaccurate statement in the published report, indicates that the statistical analysis of variance involved three variables: (1) motivating condition (interesting task interrupted, uninteresting task interrupted), (2) order-of-motivating-condition (interesting task interrupted first, uninteresting task interrupted first), and (3) students within order-of-motivating condition (16 students who were interrupted first from an interesting task and 16 students who were interrupted first from an uninteresting task). Motivating condition is considered as a "within subjects variable" because the two conditions being compared (interesting task interrupted, uninteresting task interrupted) involve the same 32 students. Variables (2) and (3) are "between subjects variables" because the comparison of the two orders and the comparison among the students each involves different subjects.

RESULTS

MOTIVATING CONDITION.   The F for this variable was 51.56 and was significant beyond the .01 level. The extent of this motivational condition effect was shown by the fact that the mean number of responses produced under the "uninteresting" condition was 57.09 whereas the mean number produced under the interesting condition was 32.09. Likewise, as shown in Table 1, the extent of the motivational effect appeared to hold equally at all age levels and for all three creativity measures despite changes in the absolute magnitudes of the mean scores.

Other results indicative of the extent of motivational effects came from the analysis of unique responses. Under the "uninteresting" condition the mean number of unique responses was 9.58 whereas it was only 3.0 under the "interesting" condition. The pervasiveness of the motivational effect was also shown by the fact that of the 32 children tested, only 2 gave fewer responses under the "uninteresting" than under the "interesting" condition. These were, moreover, among the youngest children for whom letter and number skill practice might still have had some intrinsic interest. No differences were found between black, white or Puerto Rican children nor were there significant sex differences with respect to the motivational factor.

ORDER OF MOTIVATING CONDITION.   The F for this variable was 2.14 and was non significant.

Table 1
Mean Scores for Three Creativity Measures and Four Age Groups Under Two Motivating Conditions

		Test					
		Class Concept		Alternate Uses		Similarities	
Age Group	N	I*	UI**	I	UI	I	UI
5– 6	(8)	8.25	16.38	7.50	13.13	7.13	11.38
7– 8	(8)	8.25	19.38	8.00	15.38	9.88	15.75
9–10	(8)	13.38	28.13	11.13	21.00	12.25	19.13
11–12	(8)	17.63	32.55	12.00	19.50	13.13	18.00

* I = Interesting Condition
** UI = Uninteresting Condition

GROUPS UNDER ORDER OF MOTIVATING CONDITION. The F for this variable was 1.20 and was non significant.

CRITICS' NOTE:

By "Groups Under Order of Motivating Condition" the investigators must mean students within order-of-motivating condition, and a significance test of this variable is not possible given the design used in the study.

DISCUSSION

These results seem to support the hypothesis that performance on at least some "creativity" measures is very much influenced by the ongoing activities interrupted by the test procedures. When children were temporarily removed from an "uninteresting" activity to which they knew they had to return, they were almost twice as "creative" as when they knew they would return to an "interesting" activity. This finding held equally true for boys and girls, for children at different age levels and for children from different ethnic groups. While these findings clearly do not disprove the creativity-intelligence dichotomy suggested by Getzels and Jackson (1962) and by Kogan and Wallach (1965), they do indicate that at least some putative measures of "creativity" are extraordinarily susceptible to motivational context effects.

CRITICS' NOTE:

The creativity-intelligence dichotomy is the separation of creativity and intelligence into distinct traits so that being highly intelligent does not necessarily mean being creative and vice versa.

Our results need, of course, to be replicated with other tests of creativity as well as with measures of many different skills and abilities. The effects of different motivating conditions and the resistance of children with different personalities and styles to context effects also needs to be explored. Even without this additional data, however, our results highlight the importance of considering motivational context effects whenever we evaluate psychological or educational test performance. We certainly claim no priority in pointing out the significance of such effects for test performance since their relevance has been emphasized by theorists as diverse as Brunswik (1956), Hull (1952), Lewin (1935) and Rotter (1954). Likewise, a few other recent studies have already shown the effects of motivation upon test performance (e.g., Zigler & Butterfield, 1968). All that we wish to stress is that the results of studies such as Zigler & Butterfield's and our own point to the need for more systematic exploration of the effects of motivational contexts on psychological, and particularly educational, assessment.

REFERENCES

BRUNSWIK, E. *Perception and the representative design of experiments.* Berkeley: University of California Press, 1956.

CRONBACH, L. J. Intelligence? Creativity? A parsimonious reinterpretation of the Wallach-Kogan data. *American Educational Research Journal,* 1968, 5, 491–512.

HULL, C. *A behavior system.* New Haven: Yale University Press, 1952.

LEWIN, K. *A dynamic theory of personality.* New York: McGraw Hill, 1935.

ROTTER, J. B. *Social learning and clinical psychology.* New York: Prentice-Hall, 1952.

WALLACH, M., & KOGAN, N. *Modes of thinking in young children.* New

York: Holt, Rinehart and Winston, 1965.

Zigler, E., & Butterfield, E. C. Motivational aspects of changes in IQ test performance of culturally deprived nursery school children. *Child Development*, 1968, 39, 1–14.

C R I T I Q U E

ORIENTING QUESTION OF APPRAISAL

Any study will probably contain *key* weaknesses and strengths as well as several more minor ones. By key, we mean those aspects of the study upon which the value of the work rests most heavily, and without which the study would be reduced markedly in worth. In an empirical study such as this one, *key* areas include: (A) quality of reasoning from problem statement to data to conclusions and implications; (B) methods of work (including instrumentation, design, and analysis); and (C) defense of the significance of the problem. Provide a critique of the key aspects of the study which emphasizes its key flaws and is organized into the three areas just identified. Do not concern yourself at this stage with key strengths of the study.

A.   REASONING FROM PROBLEM TO DATA TO CONCLUSIONS

Background Considerations:[1]

"Motivation and Creativity: The Context Effect," is similar to the vast majority of empirical investigations in education in that the purpose of the research is to discover and to explain relationships between variables. How these variables are defined and described is therefore crucial to the value of any such investigation.

The variables of this study are described at varying levels of abstraction. At a level close to the events, the variables are referred to as the kind of task interrupted (i.e., crossing out n's and 6's, or activities indicated by the teacher as interesting) and as the total number of responses and total

---

[1] Not expected to have been stated in a model critique but offered here for pedagogical purposes.

number of unique responses to several specific questions. At the highest level of abstraction, context and creativity are the variables being related, and motivation is seen as the construct (or abstract "mechanism") which explains the relationship.

The import of a scientific study increases greatly when an investigation is concerned with variables at higher levels of abstraction. There are two related reasons for this point. First, predictions which cover a wider range of observables are possible. Thus, for example, if a relationship is described in terms of creativity, then we can predict the relation to hold for other valid measures of creativity. On the other hand, if a relationship is examined in terms of number of uses of a newspaper, then we have a poorer basis for predicting performance with other kinds of measures. The more specific the terms of the examination, the more specific and therefore limited will be the valid applications. Secondly, the use of constructs helps us to explain the reasons for the relationship. If we want to understand the reasons for a relationship, if we want to know the extent of this relationship, and if we want to know how to allow for this relationship in the practice of education, it is important to set the observed relationship into an explanatory system or theory. Some of these ideas are illustrated by Figure 1.

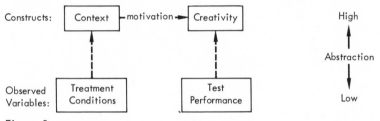

Figure 1
Variables considered in the present study and their professed interrelationship.

The importance of a study is greatly enhanced when it rises beyond providing the relation between observed variables and yields an inferred relation among constructs. But the validity of this inferred relation among constructs depends in turn upon the validity of the observed variables used to measure the constructs and upon the adequacy of the intervening constructs. Consequently, following is an assessment of the *context, creativity,* and *motivation* constructs as they are involved in the study.

Context:

In the broadest sense used in this study, "context" is seen as, "the ongoing activities interrupted by the test procedures." Other statements in the study lead one to believe that a defining property of the independent variable is the knowledge of the child that he will be returned to the task designated as "interesting" or "uninteresting." But it is not clear, when we

Condition	Before Testing		After Testing
Interesting	Interesting Activity	T E S	Resume pretesting activity — i.e., return to interesting task
Uninteresting	Cross out n's and 6's	T	Resume pretesting activity — i.e., return to crossing out n's and 6's

Figure 2
Research Design of the Present Study

interpret the results, whether differences in scores are to be attributed to some perceived contrast between past activity and present test-taking tasks, or to anticipation of some future experience. This difficulty is illustrated by Figure 2.

The difference in test performance under the two conditions might be due to the nature of the interrupted before-testing task (as the investigators suggest) or to the differential pull of the anticipated post-testing activities. For example, students in the uninteresting condition might have performed better on the tests *not* because they were happy to get out of an unpleasant task but because they persisted on the test to delay their return *to* the unpleasant task. The study design does not permit one to assess which context (the pre-testing or the post-testing) is the more important.

Motivation:

The investigators appear to have been too quick to infer that motivation is the appropriate construct to be used to explain the differential test performance. Other concepts which could explain the results include need for novelty, desire to return to a pleasant state, drive for optimal stimulation, and so forth. Still other concepts are suggested by the vast literature dealing with work conditions and production, including research on the Ziegarnik effect (the ability to recall unfinished tasks more than completed ones).

It is possible to argue that all the additional concepts being suggested are really what is meant by motivation—that is, that motivation is any drive, desire, or need. Such a concept of motivation is so broad and pervasive that it can be used to "explain" just about everything and, consequently, explains nothing. There is no way to distinguish motivating from nonmotivating contexts that is independent of test performance.

Creativity:

There is no attempt made to show that the tests employed are adequate tests of creativity. In fact, this *task* is disavowed:

It is not our intention here to deal with the issue of whether these tests measure "creativity" or something else. In this regard we tend to side with Cronbach who argues that "creativity" is too value laden and that names for particular tests should be used to designate the measure in question [p. 116].

This move on the part of the investigators succeeds in insulating the argument from the objection that creativity is not really measured by the tests, but the price of this success is the triviality of the conclusion. We can only conclude that there is a relation between context and some test scores rather than between context and creativity.

However, in spite of the quotation cited above, the investigators believe themselves to be dealing with creativity. In numerous places in the text, as well as in the title and the abstract, the investigators refer to the dependent variable as the creativity measures. Further, the most plausible reason for lumping together the scores of the three tests when drawing conclusions is that the three tests are measures of the same thing, presumably creativity.

The investigators are trying to have it both ways. They want to eat their cake (protect themselves from the objection that creativity is not really measured by the tests) and have it too (use "creativity measures" in the discussion and conclusions).

B. METHODS OF WORK

At this point in the review, we shall consider as the variables of interest the kind of task interrupted and the score on selected tests. Even at this low level of abstraction, three aspects of the research procedure hinder our interpretation of the relationship found: namely, the atypical character of the interrupted tasks, especially the uninteresting one; the inadequate description of the testing situation; and the use of a special school (WOIS) as the locus for the research.

Atypical Character of the Interrupted Tasks:

An immediate, practical result of the discovery of a context effect would be to alert the educational practitioner and researcher to the need to be concerned with the activity a child is engaged in prior to any testing situation. By using tasks seen as unrepresentative of the school situation (such as crossing out letters and numbers) the investigators reduce the likelihood that their findings will have relevance to other situations.

In defense of the investigators, it is sometimes wise to attempt to obtain the relationship desired using extreme conditions which, in this case, would be very boring and very interesting tasks. If the effects are not evident given extreme conditions, the investigator can feel quite safe in concluding the independent variable is not an important determiner of test performance in a more typical situation. If the effects are evident under extreme conditions, then future research can be directed toward the assessment of the effect in a variety of more realistic situations.

Inadequate Description of the Testing Situation:

There is a lack of information about the conduct of the creativity testing. The reader needs assurance that the testing conditions were identical under the two motivating conditions. Were the tests administered in a group situation (with the two motivation conditions separate) so that if some child were brave enough to get up and leave others might follow? What subtle cues about how long the children could work on the task may have been present? What were the children told about how long they could work on the tests, and were these instructions consistent with instructions usually given for such tests? Did the children think that if they "finished" early they could (or had to) return early to the task which had been interrupted? In short, there are far too many unanswered questions about the administration of the tests. The entire difference in test scores under the two conditions might be explained by the factors just identified.

Use of a Special School:

The importance of the nature of the interrupted task might not have been so marked had the study been conducted in a more typical school setting. The child in a special school may view the interesting and uninteresting activities as quite different in kind, and thus capable of producing marked differences in test performance. In a regular school, the variety of tasks which could be interrupted by testing would likely differ by degree rather than by kind—in fact the testing situation might be seen as an enjoyable diversion regardless of the task interrupted. We do not claim that such speculation on our part is correct; we only remind you that studies conducted in a very special situation may not generalize beyond it.

Note about Analysis:

Although a more adequate analysis of the data could have been performed, we doubt that our interpretation of results would have been much changed. A great many readers cited the use of only 32 pupils as a weakness of the study. We were not bothered by this sample size for two reasons. First, since each pupil was tested under two conditions, the effective sample size was greater than 32. Second, large samples are desired to help insure that real differences in conditions will be detected and not attributed to chance. However, a larger sample was not needed because the results of the present study were statistically significant even with the "small" sample used. (The specific questions and answers section of these appraisal materials deals, in part, with data analysis and interpretation.)

C. SIGNIFICANCE OF THE PROBLEM

One student, in appraising the research problem, argued:

> This study has very little educational significance. The primary reason is that they sought to demonstrate something which is already well accepted by psychologists and educators. It should surprise no one to find that level of motivation has an effect on the performance on a test which is at least partially scored on the basis of number of responses emitted.

The investigators themselves admit that others have shown the effect of motivation on test performance. The present study, however, deals with a motivational context of special interest to educators—namely, what the child was doing before taking the tests. It seems to us very important to know whether scores on tests such as those given in this study can be influenced to such a large extent by something as seemingly innocuous as the nature of the activity preceding the test administration.

Thus, we view the research *problem* to be significant. Because of the many concerns discussed above, however, we feel that the chief value of the study *as conducted* is to remind and caution us that particular attention to context is required when testing for creativity. The findings are provocative enough to warrant additional research on the question.

Specific Questions[2]

1. QUESTION:

The ". . . study was suggested by some unexpected findings that we encountered in our evaluation of the innovative educational program.

---

[2] The order of these questions is the same as the paragraph sequence of the published paper.

. . ." Is it legitimate to develop research from unexpected findings? Explain why you answered as you did.

1. ANSWER:

Yes, it is legitimate to develop research from an unexpected finding. A puzzling observation, an anomaly, or an unusual situation has often been the precursor of significant research. What is unexpected is, of course, a function of what is expected. In this case the *educational* expectation of increased creativity for children in a school setting stimulating inquiry and free choice was not upheld. The educators expected these children to be more, not less, creative than children in traditional schools.

Every situation has its idiosyncratic aspects. If one looks at enough features in a given situation, one or more of the observables is apt to look unusual by chance alone. Thus, although a puzzlement in one situation might well stimulate further study in an effort to seek replication or explanation of the phenomena, the first occurrence of a puzzlement should not be taken too seriously in and of itself. All perplexities are not worthy of serious further investigation.

STUDENT RESPONSE.   Unexpected findings "suggest that some important variables had not been considered or that there is some flaw in the experimental design."

OUR REPLY.   A good point. Before rushing out to seek replication of an unexpected finding, the researcher should reexamine all the procedures of the study which resulted in such phenomena in search of "flaws" which may *alone* account for the puzzling observation.

2. QUESTION:

The unexpected findings which motivated the present study resulted from a comparison of World of Inquiry School children with children selected, "from names on the waiting list for acceptance into WOIS." In this earlier evaluation of the WOIS and its effect on creativity do you approve of matching the experimental group children with children from the waiting list, or do you think the investigators should have selected the control children randomly from the public schools regardless of whether they were on the waiting list? Why?

2. ANSWER:

When comparisons are to be made, validity can be maximized if the comparison groups are as similar as possible except for the variables to be examined. If the two groups of school children were different before the one group attended the WOIS, then it is difficult to separate these initial differences from the effects of the WOIS. Of the two choices given in Question 2, taking control children from the waiting lists appears to be more valid. We can infer that such children are more likely to come from a home environment more similar to the actual WOIS children than children whose parents chose to send them to public schools.

Of course, the answer to Question 2 would be different if there were only a few children on the waiting list (and thus obtaining a good match with the WOIS children would be impossible) or if there is some systematic bias in the way in which the children who were made to wait were different from those who were accepted immediately. Thus, before giving a firm answer to Question 2, it would be helpful to know why some children were accepted and some children were made to wait. In the absence of a differential selection policy, we support the investigators' tactic of choosing controls from the waiting list group.

STUDENT RESPONSE.   The investigators should have chosen the control group randomly from the general population to, "give more credence to the generalizability of the study." Further, "those on the waiting list are a special population, perhaps more 'creative' (or motivated) than the average public school student."

OUR REPLY.   Our question refers to an earlier study which had produced the unexpected findings regarding "creativity." The purpose of that earlier study was to evaluate the WOIS. It was therefore necessary to use children who were as similar as possible to the WOIS children so that the differences between the two groups of students could be attributed to the WOIS experiences rather than other factors. To be sure, the students in the WOIS may be atypical and the ratings of effectiveness of the WOIS may not generalize to a more typical student population. But for the rather specific purpose of determining if the WOIS itself had any impact, it is necessary that the comparison group be as atypical (in the same ways) as the students in the school. A good available source for a control group was the WOIS waiting list, the source actually used.

STUDENT RESPONSE.   One student wrote,

It seems to me that the choice of control group depends on the question the researchers wanted to be able to answer. If the question was, Are children in the WOIS more "creative" than children in public schools?, then the control group should be chosen randomly. However, such a question would not tell us anything about the effect of the WOIS curriculum on encouraging "creativity" in its students. Children on the waiting list, however, have already been admitted to the school, and therefore ought to be more "similar," by whatever criteria the WOIS uses for admission, to the WOIS school population than a random sample of public school pupils. Thus, if WOIS pupils performed better on the battery than potential WOIS pupils, one would be in a position to infer that, for children likely to meet WOIS standards, the WOIS curriculum does promote "creativity" to a greater degree than does the public school curriculum.

OUR REPLY.   We agree.

3.   QUESTION:

The investigators state, "Inasmuch as each child who participated in the study served as his own control, we made no attempt to control for or to equate individual differences in ability" [page 116, *Subjects*]. (a) What does it mean for a child to serve as his own control? (b) Were the researchers justified in not equating individual differences?

3a.   ANSWER:

To serve as their own control means that observations to be compared involve the same objects (usually people). In this study, the students served as their own controls since the test scores to be compared were produced by the same children—once after they were interrupted during an interesting task and once after they were interrupted during an uninteresting task.

STUDENT RESPONSE.   When a child serves as his own control, you have "a repeated measures design."

OUR REPLY.   That is correct. "Repeated measures" occurs most frequently in the statistical literature concerned with the analysis of experimental data obtained when subjects serve as their own control.

STUDENT RESPONSE.   To serve as his own control means "the behavior and responses of each child were reflected from his own personal experience," or that "children were stratified by age," or that "children were matched."

OUR REPLY.   These answers are incorrect.

3b. ANSWER:

Yes, the investigators were justified in not equating individual differences in ability. They did not wish to match students and restrict the population of children any more than was already the case by virtue of the fact that only WOIS students were involved in the study. Further, it was not necessary to pick carefully the children because of primary interest in the study was the comparison between each pupil's score under motivating condition 1 and his own score under motivating condition 2.

4. QUESTION:

Should different (but matched) children have been used in the two motivating conditions rather than exposing the same children to both conditions? Why?

4. ANSWER:

This is an extremely difficult question to answer. Any research design is a compromise. Using children as their own controls in a repeated measures design, as in this study, has both advantages and disadvantages over the design in which matched groups of children are employed. It is a trade-off.

In the case of performance measures, individual differences account for most of the variability and treatments (such as the two motivating conditions) often make *relatively* little difference. Since this is the case, it is important that differences among the individuals in the two treatment groups be as small as possible so that the relatively small treatment (context) effect will not be masked. The great advantage of the design actually used (the subjects as their own control design) is that the differences between the individuals in the two treatment groups have been minimized. Indeed, they are the same people. A proper evaluation of the motivation conditions effects would involve a comparison of the magnitude of the difference in test performance under the two conditions, with the magnitude of the "unaccounted" for differences. When the subjects are their own control, the unaccounted for differences are reduced tremendously, making us more confident of the accuracy of the treatment differences observed.

The drawback to using subjects as their own control is that such a design does not protect against what is called a differential "carry-over" effect. To illustrate this effect, assume that instead of two motivating conditions, two drugs, A and B, were used. Further assume that drug A affects performance while drug B does not, and the effect of drug A is carried over to the time that drug B is tested. Any measure of the performance of the group that received drug B second would not be a true indication of the effect of drug B alone, since drug A would still be in effect, and any conclusions would thus be in error. Since *differential* carry-over effects are unlikely in the study as actually conducted, we would support the repeated measures design actually employed by the investigators.

STUDENT RESPONSES

Using different children would have produced a tighter control on any testing or practice effect.

There was a definite possibility of contamination in the design. Being exposed to the first form of the test might well have influenced the nature of the responses to the second form.

Having to take two equivalent forms of the same test might involve a carry-over so that the child would remember and become more proficient the second time the test is taken.

Some type of learning took place during the first testing and perhaps some modifications occur between the first and second testing.

OUR REPLY. The practice or testing effect is controlled since the order in which the two treatment conditions were given was counterbalanced—half the children were first removed from an interesting task, half the children were first removed from the uninteresting task. Thus, the student responses given above are not completely accurate; they need to specify that any "contamination" or "carry-over" effect would be *differential* in nature as explained in the second paragraph of our initial answer to this question. Why would this practice effect or learning be greater (or less) going from motivating condition 1 to motivating condition 2 than going from condition 2 to 1? We know of none.

STUDENT RESPONSES. Use of the same children is preferable to employing matched groups because: (i) "there was no pretest to help make a good match," (ii) "selection bias would take place," (iii) "it is hard to equate groups," and (iv) there are "too many variables to match children."

OUR REPLY. For matching to be maximally effective, two conditions need to be met. First, matching variables highly related to the criterion measures (creativity scores in this study) need to be used. If, as implied in student response (i), such matching variables were not available, then the effectiveness of the matching strategy would be reduced. Second, random assignment to the two treatment conditions needs to be made *after* matching has taken place. This procedure protects against the selection bias referred to in student response (ii). As long as the preceding two conditions are met, matching can be highly effective and free from bias. Contrary to that implied in responses (iii) and (iv), the groups need not be equated on numerous variables.

5. QUESTION:

The investigators state (p. 116, *Subjects*) that having children from several grades and of different ages allows for greater generality of conclusions than if a more homogeneous group were used. Do you agree? Explain.

5. ANSWER:

Yes, an investigator can make broader conclusions when he has employed a variety of subject types or has done his research in a variety of research settings. This statement presupposes that the investigator has analyzed his data by these subgroups. In this study, the investigators have performed such analysis for several age groups. We are NOT saying that the same conclusions will necessarily be valid for each of the various groups and research settings, but only that given proper analysis, one will be able to make a more general set of conclusions using a heterogeneous mixture of subjects than if a homogeneous subject pool is used.

STUDENT RESPONSES

One must have adequate numbers to generalize with confidence.

Since the sample was so small, it may be difficult to generalize for several grades and different ages.

WOIS kids are not a normal group.

OUR REPLY. These points are well taken. Because of the few children in each subcategory, the likelihood is small that the investigator will be able to make statements about the differences by such subgroups with confidence. Further, the special school setting limits generalizability to such schools. Thus, while we definitely agree with the investigators' statement as provided in Question 5, at the same time we recognize that the generalizability actually achieved in the study is limited.

6. QUESTION:

The researchers should have used more than one Puerto Rican student because it is too likely that an unusual student was in some way chosen. Comment.

6. ANSWER:

If the investigators wished to generalize their results to Puerto Rican students, then clearly more Puerto Rican students are needed for this purpose. The one student may not be typical. If the researchers wish to generalize to the WOIS population (as they clearly stated they do), then one Puerto Rican, the investigators assure us, makes about the right proportion. In fact, to use many more than one such student would make the sample unrepresentative of the WOIS population and hinder attempts to make accurate generalizations about the school population.

7. QUESTION:

Do you think it was important that the investigators show the two forms of the creativity tests to be equivalent? Why?

7. ANSWER:

Although a sensible thing to do, having strict equivalence between the two forms of the tests was not essential. Recall that the order in which the test forms were administered was counterbalanced: that is, half the time one form was given first and half the time the other form was given first. Although not explicitly stated, we believe it reasonable to assume that half the time one form was given after the uninteresting task was interrupted and half the time the other form was given after the uninteresting task. Thus, we can expect any differences in the forms (such as degree of difficulty) to balance out since neither of the motivating conditions or order-of-motivating conditions is associated with one form of the test more than the other form. In this study, equating the forms of the tests is a reasonable, but not essential, procedure to follow.

STUDENT RESPONSE. It was important to show that the two forms of the tests were equivalent because "if the difficulty of the tests were different, no conclusions could be reached." Further, "the differences found in the results could be due to the tests rather than to the treatment."

OUR REPLY. We disagree for reasons given in our initial answer to this question. Had the investigators not used a counterbalanced design, then we too would have wanted the tests equivalent.

STUDENT RESPONSES

If the tests had not been equivalent, it would not have been possible to accurately measure score changes.

It would be very difficult, if not impossible, to get accurate, valid measurement of a child's difference in scores if the difficulty of the tests were different.

OUR REPLY. It is certainly true that it is difficult to interpret an individual child's difference in the scores of two tests if the tests do not have equivalent units. But in this investigation an individual's difference score was not even computed. Each mean that was computed (see Table 1 in the research report) involved an equal number of scores on the two forms of the test.

8. QUESTION:

"The 'interesting' condition was determined by the child's own interests as indicated by the teacher." Do you approve of this procedure? Explain.

8. ANSWER:

We approve of this procedure. Of course, the investigators and readers want some assurance that the task engaged in was interesting to the child. One way to do that is to get such assurance from the child himself. Another reasonable way, it seems to us, is to trust the teachers' judgments, the procedure actually followed. Both of these approaches, asking the child himself and asking the teacher, may be subject to a bias produced when activities are reported or judged to be more interesting than they really are. (The effect of such a bias is to reduce the difference between "interesting"

and "uninteresting" activities and, consequently, to make finding significant differences between the two treatments more difficult.)

Another possible procedure would have been to parallel what was
done for the uninteresting task and put all the students in a situation the
investigators believe to be interesting to the vast majority of the children.
The problem with this procedure is that it is difficult to devise a task one
can be sure will be of high interest to a substantial number of children. The
advantage of this procedure is that it makes it possible to specify exactly
what the interesting task is and to control when the child will be ready to
begin testing.

Research design involves compromises and trade-offs. Using teachers'
judgments seems to be a reasonable choice, although we would defend as
well the other two procedures we mentioned.

STUDENT RESPONSES

> I'm not sure that the teacher can accurately determine those conditions
> which are interesting to a child.
>
> Teachers may sometimes be deceived as to a particular child's interest.
>
> It would have been better to get the child's interest from himself.
>
> I would tend to trust the involved person's judgment more.
>
> Let the child speak for himself.

OUR REPLY.   These are all reasonable responses. As indicated in our
initial answer to this question, "One way . . . is to get such assurance from
the child himself." We admit that when possible, measuring something in
the most direct available way is often the best procedure. In this case, such
a procedure would have involved going straight to the child and asking
pointedly how interested he is in a particular activity.

STUDENT RESPONSES

> I could only accept the teacher's determination of each child's interest if
> I knew exactly how she determined it. There is evidence of a lack of control
> here.
>
> I don't feel the researchers described this procedure well enough.

OUR REPLY.   These are perfectly appropriate reactions.

STUDENT RESPONSES

> I do not like the proceduce of using a teacher's judgment because this is
> not an objective method of assessing the interesting condition.
>
> No—these are subjective observations.

OUR REPLY.   By "subjective" we assume the students mean that not
all observers would agree with the teacher that the child was interested in a
particular tasks. It is true that there is a subjective element in this method
of assessment, and it is also true that when inter-judge agreement is absent,
the ratings of any one person are very likely to be invalid. Nevertheless, we

would caution against an offhand dismissal of all subjective measurements. The phenomena we may have the greatest difficulty measuring may sometimes be those most worth measuring. One must often ask whether it is better to measure well something trivial or to measure poorly something important.

9. QUESTION:

One critic of this study stated that the research assumes for its validity that all children were equally interested in the "interesting" activity. Do you agree with this statement? Why?

9. ANSWER:

We disagree. The assumption being made is that any given child will be substantially more interested in the "interesting" task than in the "uninteresting" activity. There is no reason why all children must be equally interested in their "interesting" activity, nor is it reasonable to assume they will be. The comparisons of interest are between individual performances under different conditions and not among children in the same condition.

STUDENT RESPONSES

There is no way to say that all children were equally interested.
It is very difficult to measure equal interest.
The general category, "is interested," is too gross.
The researchers did not take into account the degree of interest in the interesting activity.
The term interesting can change from day to day with this age group.

OUR REPLY.   The preceding statements seem to us to be irrelevant to the question asked. The implication in these student responses is that it would be virtually impossible to demonstrate whether or not the children were equally interested in the "interesting" activity. Although this claim may be true, Question 9 merely asks if there must be equal interest for the study to be valid.

10. QUESTION:

The researchers state that each child doing the uninteresting task "was given the same instructions about leaving to 'play games' and about returning to the ongoing activity," as the children in the interesting task condition had received. Do you approve of using the same instructions in both situations? Tell why you answered as you did.

10. ANSWER:

We do approve of using the same instructions in both situations. We want the two motivating conditions to be as alike as possible in all respects except for those variables the investigators explicitly wish to study. Such similarity makes interpretation of results less ambiguous.

STUDENT RESPONSES

The use of the words "play games" could have influenced the attitude of the child.

It does not make good common sense to instruct a child to leave an interesting activity to go play games.

The "return to ongoing activity" phrase seems to provide a key to the results, i.e., child interrupted from the uninteresting task took more time and gave more responses before returning.

OUR REPLY.   One can take exception to the wording of the instructions, as did the students whose responses are quoted above, and still believe, as we do, that the instructions should be the same for both treatment groups. (Of course "ongoing activity" will mean different things depending on which kind of task was interrupted. But this difference was precisely the difference the investigators wanted to study.)

11. QUESTION:

In order to support the claim that the interesting and uninteresting tasks indeed held those qualities for the children tested, the investigators reported their qualitative impressions of the students' feelings about being interrupted; e.g., "That the ongoing activity was indeed interesting to the child was evidenced by the groans, grimaces and footdragging that accompanied the examiner's request" and "The children complained while doing the (uninteresting) task, some called it 'stupid,' and . . . were uniformly delighted when their participation in the games was requested." Do you approve of such impressionistic reporting in research studies of this type? Why?

11. ANSWER:

We approve of such impressionistic reporting. The researcher should be alert to make observations of all phenomena associated with the research investigation. Such observations help us to interpret the more objective data which are available. They provide a fuller picture of the research context and, in this study, lend support to the judgments about task interestedness. Of course, the investigator must be alert to the possibility of experimenter bias and to evidence which is contrary to his position as well as to that which supports his position, and to report both kinds of observations.

STUDENT RESPONSES

We do not approve of such reporting because children do not mean what they say.

Emotions could have been made for other reasons.

Children very often imitate the expressions of their peers without actually feeling the same way.

The investigators appear to have jumped to conclusions in the matter of children's behavior.

OUR REPLY. The preceding responses clearly suggest that the children's behavior should not be taken at face value and that caution should be exerted in interpreting these impressions of the children's feelings. Because the impressions may be difficult to interpret, however, does not lead us to abandon them altogether.

STUDENT RESPONSES

We do not approve of such reporting because it calls for subjective judgment.

Findings should include only quantitative measures.

Impressions are not an empirical measurement.

Reports are not objective—but interesting!

OUR REPLY. See our reply to the last set of student reactions to Question 8.

12. QUESTION:

Note the design as indicated in the paragraph on page 117 above the subheading "Design." The investigators want to claim that the kind of activity engaged in (interrupted) before taking the "creativity" tests affects test performance. How many of the following variables have been controlled; that is, which variables are ruled out by the design as alternative explanations for the differential test results found: (a) order in which the two kinds of pretest activities were interrupted; (b) form of the creativity tests; (c) sex of the child; (d) age of the child; (e) "real creativity" of the child?

12. ANSWER:

All five variables were controlled. We cannot attribute the observed differences between scores on the "creativity" tests which were taken after an interesting task was interrupted and the scores of the tests after the uninteresting task, to differences in the order in which the two kinds of pretest activities were interrupted; half the children were interrupted from the uninteresting task and the other half were interrupted from the interesting task first. Further, scores from the two forms of the test are equally represented in the two sets of scores being compared. (See Table 1.) Finally, since each child was his own control—that is, was being compared against himself—the sex, age, and other characteristics such as "real creativity" were also being controlled. The utilization of a design which rules out so many rival explanations to account for the observed differences in test scores under two different motivating conditions is one of the strengths of the present study.

STUDENT RESPONSES

No attempt was made to measure "real creativity."
No one dared to define "real creativity."
Creativity is only a function of the test used.

OUR REPLY.   Variables such as size of little toe and "real creativity" can be controlled in an experiment even if measurements of these variables are not made or are not possible. One way to do this is by random assignment to treatment groups. Another way to control ability and personality characteristics is to administer the different treatments to the same person —the technique actually used by the investigators. Since the same people are involved in the two conditions, one cannot claim that the reason for differences in test scores between treatments is because the subjects in one condition were older, had more "real creativity," or had longer little toes.

STUDENT RESPONSES

I don't know what you mean by "real creativity."

The concept "real creativity" confuses me.
What the hell does "real creativity" mean?

OUR REPLY. We too do not know what "real creativity" means. We used this vague term to emphasize the point that it doesn't matter what such terms mean (for purposes of the issues discussed in this question) since each child is being compared to himself/herself. It is in this sense that we say that "real creativity" has been controlled; it has been ruled out as an explanation for the finding of treatment difference.

13. QUESTION:

Competent critiques of experiments require the reviewer to comprehend fully the research design. Especially when several variables are used, many readers find it useful to construct schematic diagrams to serve as a visual reminder of the experimental set-up. For example, if three students (S_1, S_2, and S_3) received treatment M_1 and three other students received treatment M_2, this arrangement might be pictured as shown in equivalent Figures 13–1 and 13–2.

For the present study, consider how the design used for the analysis of variance calculations might be illustrated. First, review the Critics' Note on page 118. Second, pick which one(s) of the four schematic diagrams below correctly display(s) the design used.

You do not need to know anything about analysis of variance to answer this question. You do need to know that M_1 was used to represent the interesting motivation condition and M_2 the uninteresting motivation condition. Further, O_1 and O_2 represent the two orders in which the motivating conditions were presented; S_1 to S_{32} the 32 students; and the symbol X a score on the dependent variable, a creativity measure. Note: symbols to differentiate the two sexes, the two test forms, and the four age groups were not needed as these three variables were not included in the analysis of variance calculations. Also, for ease of representation, the dots are used to signify the omission of some of the students and their scores.

(a)

		M_1	M_2
O_1	S_1	X	X
	⋮	⋮	⋮
	S_{16}	X	X
O_2	S_{17}	X	X
	⋮	⋮	⋮
	S_{32}	X	X

(b)

	O_1		O_2	
	M_1	M_2	M_1	M_2
	$S_1 \cdots S_8$	$S_9 \cdots S_{16}$	$S_{17} \cdots S_{24}$	$S_{25} \cdots S_{32}$
	X⋯X	X⋯X	X⋯X	X⋯X

(c)

	O_1			O_2		
	S_1	⋯	S_{16}	S_{17}	⋯	S_{32}
M_1	X	⋯	X	X	⋯	X
M_2	X	⋯	X	X	⋯	X

(d)

	M_1		M_2	
	O_1	O_2	O_1	O_2
S_1	X	X	X	X
S_2	X	X	X	X
⋮	⋮	⋮	⋮	⋮
S_{31}	X	X	X	X
S_{32}	X	X	X	X

13. ANSWER:

Diagrams 13a and 13c are equivalent and correct ways to illustrate the analysis of variance design which was used. In both diagrams note that a different set of 16 students belongs to each order-of-motivating condition. (In technical jargon, the variable "student" is *nested* within the variable "order-of-motivating condition.") Further, note that each person provides scores under both motivating conditions. (In technical jargon, the variable "student" is *crossed* with "motivating condition.")

Diagram 13b is not a correct representation because each student is shown receiving only one of the two motivating conditions and as contributing but one (rather than two) scores on each dependent variable. Design 13d has each student contributing four scores on each dependent variable and has him receiving the motivating conditions under both orders. It too is incorrect.

14. QUESTION:

On page 117, under the subheading "Design," the researchers mention both an age effect and an "age by motivational condition interaction effect." If there were an age effect in this study, it would mean that the average creativity test scores for the several age groups differed—that children of different ages, as a group, did not do equally well on the creativity tests.

One of the key concepts of empirical research is that of the interaction between two variables. What would have to be true about the creativity test scores of the children if there was an "age by motivational condition interaction effect"? (The purpose of this question and the discussion to follow is to help you be clear about the meaning of the term *interaction*, rather than to ask you about your opinion whether it is reasonable to expect such an interaction.)

14. ANSWER:

The presence of an age by motivational condition interaction effect would mean that the differences in creativity test performance under the two motivating conditions would vary among the several age groups. In other words, such an interaction effect would mean that the differences in the effect (on test performance) of the kind of activity interrupted depends upon the age of the child involved.[3]

STUDENT RESPONSES

Interaction between motivational condition and age occurs when motivational condition affects each age differently.

It would tell that the effect that motivational condition had was not the same for all age levels.

The older the child the greater the difference between the two test scores.

Each age group's amount of score change (under the two conditions) is different from that of each of the other group's.

OUR REPLY.   These responses are essentially correct.

STUDENT RESPONSES

If there was an age by motivational condition effect, the scores would differ depending on the age of the child.

As one grows older, his creativity scores increase (go higher) or vice versa.

The older the child, the higher the test scores would be.

The scores would vary from age to age.

---

[3] For a further discussion of the concept of interaction, hear Jason Millman, *Statistical Interactions: Their Nature and Importance.* Washington, D.C.: American Educational Research Association, Cassette Tape Series B, No. 5, 1971.

OUR REPLY. These responses are incorrect. They describe what would be true if there were an age effect, but they do not describe an interaction effect between age and motivational condition on test score.

15. QUESTION:

(a) What dependent variables were used in the study? (b) Is it a good idea to use more than one dependent variable in a study? Why?

15a. ANSWER:

The dependent variables are those which are affected by the values of the other variables and whose values "depend" upon the conditions under which an investigation is conducted. In this study, the dependent variables are measured by the creativity tests, for the effect on such tests is of interest. More specifically, three separate creativity tests were used and two scores—number of responses and number of unique responses—were computed for each test. However, for use in the analysis of variance, the researchers added the number of responses from all three tests to form a new composite variable. They also computed a total uniqueness score by adding the unique response scores for the three tests. These latter scores are reported in the second column on page 118.

STUDENT RESPONSES

The dependent variables were the interesting tasks and the uninteresting tasks.

Conditions before testing, interesting or uninteresting.

Motivation.

OUR REPLY. These responses are not correct. The nature of the interrupted task (that is, the motivating condition) was the primary INDEPENDENT variable of the study whose effect on the dependent variables was being studied.

STUDENT RESPONSES

Score change was the dependent variable.

The changed scores between the two tests.

OUR REPLY. It is reasonable to think of the dependent variables as change scores on the several indices of creativity. For example, the statistical test of the difference between creativity scores under the two motivating conditions is equivalent to the statistical test of whether the mean change score is zero.

15b.   ANSWER:

Although there are some inconveniences and possibilities for contamination, on balance we approve strongly of multiple dependent variables in a study since it is possible that the effects being sought will show up for some dependent variables and not for others. A study of the pattern of these results can provide a more complete insight into the phenomena under consideration.

STUDENT RESPONSES

Using more than one dependent variable is a good idea because it gives a better check on treatment effects.

Yes, you have a stronger case for generalizability when you use more than one test.

Yes, it is well to use more dependent variables in order to get more information.

Yes, especially with a concept like creativity where a definite universal instrument is not available.

Using several dependent measures is an efficient way of collecting a lot of data at once. Also, if the variable measured is not well defined, as is the case here, using more than one measure provides a way of converging on the concept under consideration.

OUR REPLY.   We concur with these reasons.

16.   QUESTION:

On page 118 under the main heading "Results," is written: *"Motivating Condition.* The *F* for this variable was 51.56 and was significant beyond the .01 level." (a) What was significant? (b) What does it mean to be "significant beyond the .01 level?" (If you have not studied statistics, you probably will not be able to answer these questions. Nevertheless, you should study our discussion for it is intended to help you understand frequently used statements like the one quoted above.)

16a.   ANSWER:

Strictly speaking it is the value of *F* which is significant. (*F* refers to a statistic computed as part of the analysis of variance.) Also, the 25 point difference in mean number of responses produced under the uninteresting (57.09) and interesting (32.09) conditions was "significant" in the statistical sense of the word.

16b. ANSWER:

If the null hypothesis of no difference in the means of test scores which could be obtained under the two motivating conditions were true, then the probability of obtaining the size differences reported in Table 1 (or differences even more extreme) is less than one chance in a hundred. In this case, significance means rejecting the notion of equal group means in the population. "Beyond the .01 level" means that the probability is less than (i.e., "beyond") .01 that sample results as extreme as those found would occur if the no difference hypothesis were true.

STUDENT RESPONSES

To be significant beyond the .01 level means that only 1% of the time will such (extreme) results occur because of chance or sampling error.

The probability is less than 1% that the observed data (or those more extreme) could have occurred only by chance.

OUR REPLY. These interpretations are correct. Note that they discuss the probability of the observed data occurring if something (chance alone operating) were really true. A statement of a student that "the (expression) indicates such results as these would happen less than 1% of the time" is correct as far as it goes—but it needs the qualifying phrase, if chance alone were operating, to be completely correct.

STUDENT RESPONSES

Significant beyond the .01 level means that the probability of results having been influenced by chance is less than 1%.

The probability that chance happened is less than 1%.

Less than 1% possibility that results were obtained by chance.

It means that less than .01 of the time, chance will be the only causative factor.

OUR REPLY. The preceding responses and their variants are the most frequently made, and they are not correct. Equally incorrect are statements that you are 99% confident that chance alone was operating—e.g., "the chance that differences in creativity scores are caused by manipulation of motivating conditions, and not by chance, is at least 99/100."

The difficulty with these responses is that they state the probability that something is really true beyond the sample results. (In this classical use of probability, either chance alone was operating or it was not—the probability is either 1 or 0.) You should carefully compare our initial answer to this question and the first set of student responses which we said were correct to the set of student responses directly above which we labeled as incorrect. The former give the probability of sample results given a correct chance-alone hypothesis (the correct interpretation); the latter give the probability of the chance-alone hypothesis being correct given the sample results which were found (the incorrect interpretation).

17. QUESTION:

Although admitting that norms are not required to test the hypothesis of the study, one student reader suggested that if national norms for the creativity tests had been reported by the investigators, we could see whether the uninteresting task was responsible for better-than-expected performance or, alternatively, whether the interesting task was responsible for poorer-than-expected performance. Do you agree? Explain.

17. ANSWER:

We do not agree. Because the WOIS students in the study may not be typical of the test standardization group, we cannot determine how the WOIS students might have scored, without any unusual pretest conditions, compared with a norm group. Their mean score might have been either lower or, more likely, higher than the norm group mean. Since we cannot establish that the norm group mean and the WOIS group mean under normal testing conditions would be the same, any comparison of the test results with norm group scores would be a meaningless endeavor. For example, if the uninteresting task group scores above the norm group mean and the interesting task group scores at the norm group mean, it could be that: (*a*) the uninteresting task spurred the students on to better-than-expected performance or that, (*b*) the interesting task lowered the performance below the level expected of WOIS students.

Somewhat aside, it might have been useful to have a third matched group from the same WOIS population take the tests under standardized administration conditions. Such a third group (*a*) could help determine if the uninteresting task had a positive effect, the interesting task a negative effect, or both, and (*b*) could provide data on the typicalness of the WOIS children on the creativity measures. However, an investigator cannot study all the questions he/she might like to, or, in a single study, cannot gather all the data of some benefit. Priorities must be made. We do *not* criticize the researchers of this study for failure to include such a control group.

STUDENT RESPONSES

What conditions were the norms obtained under? Conditions of motivation were probably not considered for the norms; therefore, they are not relevant to this experiment.

No, norms would not be useful because they were not derived under the same experimental conditions as the study.

OUR REPLY.   These students seem to miss the point of the question. It is recognized that the context of testing was different between that found in the study and that present when the tests were normed. The question asked whether, therefore, the difference between the WOIS and norm results could tell us anything about how the context of testing affects test performance—specifically whether it tended to raise the results (of one of the motivating groups) or lower the results of another. For the reasons given in our initial answer, we concluded that the norm information would not be of much value.

18.   QUESTION:

On page 118, column 2, the researchers speculate why, contrary to all the other children, two children gave more responses when taken away from an interesting task than when taken away from an uninteresting task. Should they have made this kind of speculation in a paper of this type? Comment.

18.   ANSWER:

Definitely. The purpose of research is to explain phenomena. It is quite proper, in fact laudatory, that the investigators share their insights with the reader even though they cannot prove their claims. It is considered good research form to separate speculation and after-the-fact opinionating from the line of theorizing to which the study was specifically directed. The investigators have clearly made this division.

STUDENT RESPONSE

Yes, it seems reasonable to suggest a possible reason for a result that doesn't "fit." It might lead to further investigation, just as their original speculation led to this study.

OUR REPLY.   We agree.

STUDENT RESPONSES

This speculation was not necessary, especially since the investigators did not state any attempt toward age-group analysis.

. . . suggests that age should have been one of the variables.

Although the age variable was not incorporated into the design . . .

If they want to replicate, they may want to consider the age factor.

OUR REPLY.   Although age was not included in the analysis of variance calculation, the creativity test data associated with the two motivation conditions reported in Table 1 were further subdivided by age groups. Contrary to the student responses quoted above, the age factor was a variable in the design and was considered.

19.   QUESTION:

On page 118, column 2, the investigators write: ". . . nor were there significant sex differences with respect to the motivational factor." To what kind of significance (statistical or practical) are the investigators referring here? Or are we unable to tell?

19.   ANSWER:

The type of significance is not clear. Not enough information is given to answer the question with certainty. The researchers could be referring to statistical significance although they do not report conducting any significance test of such an hypothesis. On the other hand, the investigators could merely have noted the differences in mean scores under the two motivating conditions for each sex and concluded, without conducting a statistical test, that the differences of these differences were not of practical significance (that is, were not very important).

STUDENT RESPONSES

(a)   I think the significance they were referring to is the fact that girls tend to do better on tests requiring verbal responses.

(b)   No significance differences is an interesting observation to make because I would guess girls to be more creative than boys.

(c)   I assumed the researchers were saying that there was no difference in the motivation of boys and girls.

OUR REPLY.   These responses illustrate a confusion about the differences being discussed. Regarding response (*c*), differences in motivation are not involved for motivational condition (type of task interrupted) is an independent—not a dependent—variable which is assigned to the children. By no significant sex differences *with respect to the motivational factor* the investigators are referring to a lack of *interaction* between sex and motivational condition. That is, they are not claiming that boys and girls scored about the same on the creativity tests (as implied in response *b*), but rather that the *differences* under the two motivating conditions for boys and the corresponding *differences* for girls were themselves not significantly different.

20. QUESTION:

In the abstract and on page 119, the researchers state that one group was almost twice as creative as the other. What assumption about test scores is necessary to justify this remark?

20. ANSWER:

The assumption is that stating twice as many uses for objects (the results reported by the investigators) means having twice the creativity. In more technical language, the assumption is that the test scores measure creativity at the measurement level called a ratio scale. The sentences in question would have been more accurate and less misleading if they had been worded either in terms of "twice as many responses" or "significantly more 'creative.'"

STUDENT RESPONSE.   Many students said that "the tests must be valid measures of creativity."

OUR REPLY.   This is correct, as far as it goes. More than validity is required, however, before we can make the twice-as-creative interpretation. Our thermometer is a valid measure of temperature, but we would not say a reading of an outside temperature of 6° indicates twice the heat of a reading of 3°. Zero degrees does not indicate absolute lack of heat just as zero number of responses on the creativity test does not indicate absolute lack of creativity.

STUDENT RESPONSE

The standardized norms of a test have to be known before one can make the assumption that one group was twice as creative as the other.

OUR REPLY.   We disagree. Although having norms would permit us to make a comparison with the performances of such a standardized sample, they would not, by some mysterious process, give to the scores this ratio scale property about which we spoke.

21. QUESTION:

In the discussion section on page 119, the investigators imply relevance of their study to the creativity-intelligence dichotomy. Is their study relevant in this regard? (See the second Critics' Note on page 119.)

21. ANSWER:

We know of no relevance of this work to the creativity-intelligence dichotomy and are at a loss to explain why any reference to it was made.

STUDENT RESPONSES

While this study does not disprove the creativity-intelligence dichotomy, it implies that motivating factors may be as important or more important in generating creative responses.

Perhaps the study has relevance to the creativity-intelligence dichotomy in the sense that a relationship between creativity and intelligence should take motivation into account.

Tangentially relevant to the larger problem of defining "creative ability" distinct from "intelligent behavior."

OUR REPLY. Although the above student responses have merit, at best they only make a case for a most indirect kind of relevance that the study might have to the question of whether intelligence and creativity are distinct traits.

22. QUESTION:

What would you say is the main conclusion of the study?

22. ANSWER:

The investigators would probably claim that their main conclusion is that their results: ". . . highlight the importance of considering motivational context effects whenever we evaluate psychological or educational test performance." This conclusion can be worded many ways and still retain its essence—that test performance depends upon motivation or, in less abstract terms, that the type of task engaged in prior to testing can markedly affect a child's measured creativity. Regardless which wording you prefer, because of many weaknesses (especially those discussed in the general critique) we cannot assess this study as a rigorous examination of motivational context effects.

STUDENT RESPONSE

A valid conclusion cannot be drawn from an invalid study.

OUR REPLY.   We disagree. For example, fortunetellers are frequently right, especially when predictions are made which agree with one's expectations. One student, frustrated by our answer to Question 22, said: "But I feel that we can and should consider the motivational factor in psychological testing." We feel that way, too, and would like to see additional research to test this conviction.

9

Tampering with Nature
in Elementary School Science*

Joanne Reynolds Bronars

The science program in the elementary school generally includes a unit on plant and animal life. Many such units include one or more of the following recommended learning experiences:[1]

(1) Enclosing flies, crickets, or grasshoppers in jars and cutting off the air supply in order to prove that living things need air in order to stay alive.

(2) Catching, chloroforming, and mounting insects, moths, and butterflies in order to study their structure.

(3) Withdrawing light and water from selected plants in order to prove that these are necessary factors in plant growth.

(4) Dropping acid on live meal worms in order to observe reactions to outside stimuli.

(5) Controlling the diet of white mice so that some of them will display the effects of malnutrition.

(6) Putting frogs in ice water in order to slow down bodily processes and simulate hibernation.

(7) Incubating hens' eggs, which are broken open at various stages in order to examine developing embryos.

(8) Dissecting plants, flowers, starfish, frogs, and other small creatures. The McGraw-Hill Book Company will now supply through the mail live crayfish, guppies, mice, and other small animals for use in elementary school classroom experiments and demonstrations.[2]

All of these activities involve having children control, distort, or stop the life processes of some kind of living or-

* Originally appeared in The Educational Forum, November 1968, pp. 71–75. Reprinted with permission of the publisher.

[1] See, for example, such science texts as June Lewis and Irene Potter, The Teaching of Science in the Elementary School (Englewood Cliffs, N.J.: Prentice-Hall, 1961); Wilbur Beauchamp and Helen Challand, Basic Science Handbook K-3 (Chicago: Scott, Foresman & Co., 1961); Edward Victor, Science for the Elementary School (New York: The Macmillan Co., 1965).

[2] The New York Times, March 27, 1966.

ganism in order to learn something about its functioning. Two assumptions underlie these activities: first, that the concepts and facts to be learned constitute necessary additions to the child's store of knowledge and secondly, that children learn more easily, thoroughly, and with a higher degree of interest through first-hand experiences involving direct manipulation of concrete materials.

The question as to which specific learnings should be a part of the curriculum will not be explored here, nor will any objection be raised against the general learning principle stated above. There are, however, some related assumptions regarding the acceptability of these classroom experiences which need to be examined, both in terms of their intellectual grounds and of their moral implications. Three assumptions will be examined here:

(1) School children share in the right of human beings to control and alter the natural environment in order to satisfy curiosity, add to our store of knowledge, or to make life more safe and comfortable.

For most men the realm of value deals with human values—with a concern for man's desires and needs. However, as we have increased our understanding of the ways in which man is integrally related to the web of nature, we have come to see that man's control over the natural world must be subject to limitations. Wholesale destruction or exploitation of other forms of life imperils our own life on this planet as will the uncontrollable multiplication of man as a species. Rachel Carson reminds us:

The balance of nature is not the same today as it was in Pleistocene times, but it is still there: a complex, precise, and highly integrated system of relationships between living things which cannot safely be ignored any more than the law of gravity can be defied with impunity by a man perched on the edge of a cliff. The balance of nature

is not a *status quo;* it is fluid, ever shifting, in a constant state of adjustment. Man, too, is part of this balance. Sometimes the balance is in his favor; sometimes—and all too often through his own activities—it is shifted to his disadvantage.[3]

Furthermore, sociologists, anthropologists, and others increasingly point up the fact that we are part of one human race, and that we need to discard tribal concepts in favor of a concern for the welfare of all members of the human family. It is more and more the case, then, that decisions involving the control or destruction of any form of life must be made on the basis of sober and intelligent assessment of long range and far reaching consequences.

It seems reasonable to assert that such decision making belongs in the hands of mature adults who not only possess a large body of data upon which to base their decisions, but who also are capable of being moved by what has been termed "a reverence for life." It is in childhood that such a sense of reverence will need to be developed, as well as an understanding of man's interrelatedness with nature. We need to consider the kind of school science program which will best accomplish this.

This purpose is not being served when the focus is upon experimentation with living things which have been wrenched from an ecological system. Rather, the focus might better be upon an understanding and appreciation of our world gained through *observation,* so that children, like the ancient Greeks, might behold its workings with a sense of wonder.

Focusing science study upon observation of living things in their natural habitat would require a program built upon field trips, rather than upon the importation of separate items from a site into the artificial environment of the classroom. If observations are plan-

---

[3] Rachel Carson, *Silent Spring* (New York: Fawcett World Library, 1964), p. 218.

ned carefully, children can witness all aspects of the life cycle including, if it is thought to be important, such phenomena as malnutrition and death. Children can be taught to make careful sketches of plants and animals out in the field. They can observe and record on film seasonal changes or changes in the life cycle of an organism. They can listen to woodland sounds and capture them with a tape recorder. Furthermore, children can be helped to make decisions regarding which items might be removed from a field site without disturbing its ecology (fallen leaves, but not leaves pulled from trees; abandoned nests of birds, but not those in use, etc.) as an initial stage in their understanding that there is privilege, purpose, and responsibility involved in man's control of his environment. The privilege is one to be earned by individuals possessed of emotional and intellectual maturity; the purpose must be clearly defined and justified; the responsibility must be knowingly and willingly assumed. We need to ask whether all three of these criteria have been satisfied when we allow children to cut off a grasshopper's life in a glass jar.

(2) All children do or should have similar value orientations toward forms of life which some adults consider to be worthless.

A current science text introduces an experiment involving the killing of flies and grasshoppers with the injunction, "Make sure that the children regard the animals used in the following experiments as pests and that they understand that these animals do not feel pain as humans do."[4] What is the meaning of the term 'pest'? It is generally used to designate something which causes inconvenience to the one employing the term. Some adults consider flies to be pests because they deposit germs on food or because they buzz around in an annoying way. But where

houses are well screened, flies do not pose the same kind of threat, and from an aesthetic point of view might be considered to be quite beautiful and to be appropriate subjects for poetry along with the dragon fly or the Japanese beetle. Grasshoppers may be considered to be pests because in great numbers they destroy crops. A few grasshoppers in the city, however, do not pose that kind of danger, but rather may be admired for their remarkable athletic feats. Some children may regard bees as pests because they sting; others may regard them as friends because they make honey. What is being suggested here is that the term 'pest' is a value term, not a descriptive one. We cannot describe certain living things as pests *per se,* nor can we expect that all children will or should agree with the way in which we employ the term in the classroom. All that we can do is to state a value position and invite children to consider it. The teacher's right to compel children to accept it is a moral question that needs to be explored.

Just as the concept of what constitutes a pest needs analysis, so does the concept of pain as it applies to animals. Pain is a philosophical concept, not a publicly observable phenomenon. We can only assume that other human beings feel pain as we do when they say, "I have a toothache," or when we make certain inferences from their overt behavior. Since we cannot communicate with fish, insects, trees, or grass, the question as to whether these forms of life experience anything that we could designate as pain becomes even harder to deal with. Again, we cannot assert to children in the classroom that grasshoppers feel no pain; we can only state it as a debatable assumption, and may expect that some children will not regard it as a sufficient ground for permitting experiments upon them.

The fact that a variety of attitudes, feelings, and values about living things may be expressed by children in any one class is often not recognized, much less hoped for. This writer has

---

[4] Lewis and Potter, *op. cit.,* p. 177.

asked a number of groups of college students to respond to the question, "At what point along the following continuum would it bother you to injure, kill, or dissect the form of life indicated?" The continuum consisted of the following items: grass, flowers, ants, flies, worms, goldfish, mice, cats, pigs, horses, and human beings.

There was at least one student in every group who was disturbed by the thought of trampling down grass or picking flowers. Other students ranged along the continuum which extended to those who had witnessed and were interested in various forms of surgery, including autopsies. When we examined the grounds for the feelings or attitudes expressed, they were based upon concerns such as the following:

A religious sense of the sacredness of all forms of life; aesthetic sensitivity toward all forms of life in their natural state; acute distress at the thought of inflicting pain on any living thing; revulsion at the thought of handling maimed or dead things (Sometimes this depended upon size: "I could kill or dissect a mouse but not a hamster"); emotional identification with animals that are conventionally regarded as pets; and interest in the structure and functions of organisms and in experimentation which will improve life for man.

It might be argued that it is the job of the school to change attitudes through a broadening of the child's experience, in which case the child would be compelled to participate in all of the planned classroom experiences. On the other hand, it might be argued that respect must be given to the feelings and points of view expressed by the children and genuine options accorded them regarding the activities in which they will participate. Thus the child who does not wish to kill flies or mount butterflies would not be penalized or condescended to by the teacher or by his classmates. In any case, we need to

explore with children the variety of emotional, philosophical, and religious stances that are taken toward various forms of life and examine the meanings attached to such concepts as "pest," "useful form of life," "purposeful behavior," or "consciousness."

(3) Examination of the actual object will result in better learning than the use of representative materials.

A general acceptance of the value of firsthand experience does not preclude the necessity for making some qualifications regarding specific learning experiences. For example, when students dissect a frog in order to study its internal organs, how much do they actually see? Unless a dissection is skillfully performed the organs may be mangled. If a student is numbed by revulsion, he may be blocked from an objective contemplation of the object before him. Perhaps in these cases much more could be learned from an examination of enlarged color slides or even carefully drawn diagrams. Some of the excellent models of human anatomy are becoming more widely used in schools and seem to be regarded as adequate substitutes for human corpses. When flowers are being studied, some of the large, beautifully constructed models of flower parts, which can be taken apart and reassembled, may provide a more effective means of studying about the reproductive function of the flower than an examination of actual pistils and ovaries. Some natural processes cannot really be observed at all by the naked eye, as, for example, the opening of a bud into a fully opened flower. Separate stages in the process may be witnessed, but the use of films employing time-lapse photography provides a learning experience which no amount of firsthand examination of flowers can duplicate.

What is being suggested is that we must be clear about the aim of a particular science activity and intelligent in our selection of the most effective form of learning experience, be it the actual object, photographs, diagrams, models, television viewing, or a live demonstration. If this were done, we might find that the tradition bound one-shot lesson on the dissection of a frog has little to commend it beyond the fact that it has always been a part of the syllabus.

In summary, we need to undertake a careful examination of the assumptions underlying experimentation with living things in the elementary school science program. The position is taken here that it should be the job of the elementary school to help children develop observational techniques with which to study the natural world. Furthermore, they should be helped to develop a respect for various life processes and an understanding of their own interrelatedness with nature. It is recognized that some educators may consider experimentation with living things to be a legitimate part of the science program, but it is believed that such activities must be carried out in a sensitive, intelligent manner with full awareness of the philosophical, moral, and psychological implications.

C R I T I Q U E

1. QUESTION:

Bronars is responding to the need to undertake "A careful examination of the assumptions underlying experimentation with living things in the elementary school science program." What common name or classification do we give to this kind of critical analysis?

1. ANSWER:

Usually we think of such studies as philosophical research. Somewhat aside, we would like to point out that one of the traditional tasks taken on by philosophers of education has been the examination of educational theories and practices so that the basic assumptions and values inherent in them may be uncovered and clearly displayed for all to see. The Bronars article follows this traditional form of philosophical research, as it presents an aspect of the elementary school science curriculum and probes beneath the surface of a set of particular activities to ask normative questions about what values we may inadvertently teach by engaging students in such activities.

The obvious audience to which this and a host of similar philosophical articles is addressed is the educational practitioner. Such articles force him to be reflective about his practice, not in terms of its efficiency or technical propriety, but more fundamentally in terms of its broadly human and ethical dimensions. Since the time of Socrates, philosophers have served as such "gadflies" to force public and personal reflection upon our basic values, beliefs, and attitudes, and to thereby bring us to lead the "examined life." Especially in so basic a human activity as education, such an examination is particularly significant.

2. QUESTION:

Is Bronars' article an educational research paper?

2. ANSWER:

Yes. It is a study of educational practices, but it is not primarily an empirical study (i.e., it is more theory-based than experiment-based). The predominance of empirical research in education and the consequent stress on the methodologies of such research seem to lead many people to believe that only empirical studies conforming to certain methodological norms are properly called "research." Typically, philosophical research continues the oldest tradition of research—that based on careful observation of the world and reasoned thought about it.

3. QUESTION:

One form that logical arguments about educational practice can take is the practical syllogism. This form usually has three parts: (1) the normative premise(s), i.e., a statement of what is good; (2) the empirical claims or alleged facts in the case; and (3) the value judgments or conclusions about what should be done. It is never explicitly stated in Bronars' article but one possible argument is the following:

> *Normative premise:* Reverence for life is a good thing.
> *Empirical claims:* (a) Many elementary school teaching practices in use today do not instill a reverence for life. (b) There are educational practices available which do instill a reverence for life.
> *Conclusion:* Adopt these preferred practices.

Does the fact that this argument contains normative judgments make the argument invalid?

3. ANSWER:

No. It is a valid argument. Since the conclusions follow from the premises, we say that the argument is valid. The facts as claimed or alleged, however, may not be true as stated. Logical validity is not the same concept as empirical (fact-based) validity. It is unfortunate that the language of research uses the same term, "validity," in two very distinctly different ways.

4. QUESTION:

The article contains the recommendation to change the orientation of elementary science programs from experimentaiton with living things to observation of them. Is this change necessary in the light of the normative premise, "reverence for life is a good thing"? Explain.

4. ANSWER:

No. We agree with Bronars who answered our question (personal communication) as follows:

> The normative premise is not that of unqualified reverence for life but rather the importance of a developed attitude toward nature which involves a sense of purpose and responsibility. The point is not that experimentation should not be carried on, but that when it is carried on it is for the purpose of thoughtfully conceived ends which adults have assumed responsibility for achieving. That is why I am suggesting that the focus be upon observing where *children* are concerned.

5. QUESTION:

The investigator considers three assumptions people use in support of practices that "tamper with nature." If we assume that her arguments against them are conclusive, does such a refutation of the assumptions conclusively support her main argument? Why or why not?

5. ANSWER:

No. They are logically independent. That is, a person could *either* agree *or* disagree with each assumption and still either agree or disagree with recommendations for educational practice.

Even if all three assumptions are rejected, as Bronars rejects them, a person could still agree or disagree with her educational recommendations.

6. QUESTION:

Bronars is concerned with what children learn when they have learning experiences involving the killing of flies and grasshoppers. To what kind of learning might she have appealed to support her argument?

6. ANSWER:

Many empirical researchers and educational thinkers have commented on the notion of *incidental* or collateral learning. It is always appropriate to ask what *else* children are learning when we teach them. The Bronars article stimulates us to ask if we are teaching children to disregard reverence for life when we use living organisms as subjects of experiments in school. We would expect empirical research to show that in some cases we do engender the "wrong" belief systems through such experiments.

7. QUESTION:

Does this article contain any data?

7. ANSWER:

Yes. Check page 154 where Bronars reports responses obtained from college students which indicate a continuum of attitudes toward living things, plus the concerns which justify these attitudes. She also quotes a datum from the *New York Times* about the availability of living creatures from a publishing company. She also reports other information that is properly considered data. A datum is more than a number; it is anything that serves as evidence for an assertion.

8. QUESTION:

Bronars takes exception to some current classroom practices in elementary school science. (a) Upon what sources of information does Bronars draw to describe these practices? (b) Is there any reason to doubt the validity of her description of these classroom practices? (c) Is it important that her description be valid? Explain.

8. ANSWER:

(a)   Elementary school science textbooks.

(b)   Units recommended by textbook writers may not be the ones actually used in the classroom. Observation of classrooms or reports of activities actually taking place in classrooms would be more valid indicators of classrooms practices.

(c)   Yes and no. If the practices Bronars is complaining about occur only infrequently, then the article no longer has much practical significance. On the other hand, as long as *some* teachers behave as described (which is most assuredly the case), then the validity of the article turns not on the frequency of these "objectionable" practices but on the clarity and coherence of the arguments.

9. QUESTION:

Does the information in column 1 of page 154 help Bronars to reject Assumption 2 on page 153?

9. ANSWER:

The data will help to the degree that the responses made by college students and referred to in the article will generalize to children. Bronars' data have force only to the degree that we assume children would respond in a similar way.

10. QUESTION:

Write out Bronars' definition of the word "pest." Most primary dictionary definitions call attention to the historical origin of the word and define "pest" as any organism capable of causing a fatal disease in epidemic proportions. Obviously her definition differs from the primary definition of most dictionaries. Characterize this difference and discuss its importance in terms of Bronars' argument.

10. ANSWER:

Bronars defines "pest" as "something which causes inconvenience to the one employing the term." Thus Bronars treats "pest" as an evaluative term; the primary dictionary definition is descriptive.

Bronars argues that what some adults (e.g., science textbook writers) consider to be pests and worthless, other people (such as teachers and children in their classes) may not consider as pests and, therefore, should not be harmed. This argument requires that "pest" not be considered a descriptive term (in which case there would be widespread agreement). Rather, her argument requires an evaluative definition so that "We cannot describe certain living things as pests *per se* [p. 153]." Bronars *stipulates* her definition of pest, and that this definition contains within it the evaluative phrase "inconvenience to one employing the term." She has chosen one meaning of "pest" over other meanings readily associated with the term without giving explicit reasons for rejecting the alternative (and competing) meanings. The science textbook writers would be equally justified in asserting that *for them* "pest" is a descriptive term applied to organisms that cause fatal diseases and epidemics.

However Bronars (personal communication) responds:

> While the primary dictionary definition of the term "pest" is descriptive, I wished to draw attention to the evaluative one. I agree that I should have spelled out my reasons for doing so. In the same way, however, the textbook writers need to explain their use of the term. As the experiment is set forth the fly is not killed because he is a "pest" (descriptive) but because it is

assumed that no one will object to its being used as a victim. There are other attitudes towards flies, however, as seen in some of the *Scientific American* articles on their life cycle. Here reference is made to their beauty and to other kinds of characteristics.

We might add to this by quoting Uncle Toby's reaction to flies, from *Tristram Shandy*:

—Go—says he, one day at dinner, to an over-grown [fly] which had bussed about his nose, and tormented him cruelly all dinner-time–and which, after infinite attempts, he had caught at last, as it flew by him;—I'll not hurt thee, says my Uncle *Toby*, rising from his chair, and going across the room with the fly in his hand,—I'll not hurt a hair of thy head:—Go, says he, lifting up the sash, and opening his hand as he spoke, to let it escape;—go poor devil, get thee gone, why should I hurt thee?—This world surely is wide enough to hold both thee and me.[1]

The difference between evaluative and descriptive definitions of terms is not very important with regard to Bronars' paper. It is, however, generally an important point. Too often in educational research, where the value issues continually impinge on every significant problem, we find slippage between a descriptive and evaluative definition of some key term. The shift of meanings is often very subtle and is something one should be constantly on guard to catch.

11.   QUESTION:

Bronars writes, "Pain is a philosophical concept, not a publicly observable phenomenon [p. 153, column 2]." Give reasons for accepting or rejecting this statement.

11.   ANSWER:

Here is one reason why we might want to reject the statement as it stands: The statement claims that pain is a philosophical concept. It seems to us that pain is no more a philosophical concept than it is a physical concept, or a medical concept, or a concept of ordinary human experience. It is a feeling. There are many different contexts in which the term "pain" is used to refer to this feeling. However we might want to accept the general sense of the statement because we can make a distinction between a concept

---

[1] Laurence Sterne, *The Life and Opinions of Tristram Shandy, Gentleman,* ed. and intro. Samuel Holt Monk (New York: Holt, Rinehart and Winston, 1950), pp. 96–97.

(and its sign, such as a word, a gesture, a mark) and that to which the concept refers. Concepts which are relatively rich have attached to them a cluster of criteria (sets of meaning) which we use in correctly applying the term. There is an important sense in which it is appropriate to say that we do not "see a concept." We can, however, reach agreement about what it is the concept refers to, i.e., what is observed. Thus, in common medical practice, doctors reach agreement about pain, the threshold of tolerance for pain, the effectiveness of drugs and other treatments in reducing pain, and so on.

12. QUESTION:

Bronars writes: "All we can do is to state a value position and invite children to consider it. The teacher's right to compel children to accept it is a moral question. . . . [p. 153, column 2]." Yet the tenor of her article suggests that "reverence for life" must be taught to children. Is she logically inconsistent? Why or why not?

12. ANSWER:

At first glance it might appear that she is being logically inconsistent. Bronars states as a fact (p. 153, last paragraph) that there are a variety of feelings which children have about living things. Thus, presumably, *some* could have notably tougher ideas about living things than Bronars might wish. To suggest that "reverence for life" must be taught to these tough-minded children implies that the teacher needs to go beyond merely *inviting* them to consider this value.

In fact, though, she is not being inconsistent. To suggest that something must be taught in schools does not entail the suggestion that children must be compelled to accept it.

13. QUESTION:

Bronars suggests that science study be focused on observation of living things in their natural habitat. She also suggests that learning with actual objects (i.e., living organisms) may not be as effective as learning with representative materials. Is there a contradiction in these two suggestions? Explain.

13. ANSWER:

Again, she is not being inconsistent. To explain why, we might best quote her own response (personal communication). "Reference is made to the kinds of science study that would best be carried on through the use of field observation techniques (pp. 152–153) and that would best be carried on through the use of representative materials (p. 154). There is on contradiction but rather a reference to different *kinds* of phenomena."

14. QUESTION:

What is Bronars' main question about effects of the educational practices examined in her report? Briefly sketch how this question might be answered empirically.

14. ANSWER:

The main concern of the paper seems to be the relation between certain activities in elementary science practice and two related values: (a) attitudes of children concerning reverence for life, and (b) attitudes of children toward the balance of nature.

An empirical study comparing these attitudes in children who both have and have not been exposed to the practices of elementary school science which are being questioned here might help determine the effects of these practices upon such attitudes.

However, it must be stressed that Bronars' arguments cannot be "validated" or "disproved" by any possible result of such an experiment. She wants to argue that classroom activities that involve the heedless and casual killing of living things are wrong in themselves. If we ran a test that discovered killing people did not seem to affect people's attitude toward human life we could hardly claim to have shown that killing people is all right.

10

Effects of Hierarchical Differentiation on Group Productivity, Efficiency, and Risk Taking*

Edwin M. Bridges / Wayne J. Doyle
David J. Mahan

In this paper the authors hypothesize that hierarchically differentiated groups will (1) exhibit less risk-taking behavior, (2) be less efficient, and (3) be less productive than hierarchically undifferentiated groups. To test the hypotheses, 10 hierarchically differentiated groups and 10 hierarchically undifferentiated groups formed from the staffs of 10 elementary schools were given a problem in logic. Results confirmed all three hypotheses at the analysis phase of problem-solving. Too few groups solved the problem to permit testing of the third hypothesis at the synthesis phase of problem solving.

Edwin M. Bridges is associate professor of education at the University of Chicago; Wayne J. Doyle and David J. Mahan are research associates at Washington University, St. Louis.

INTRODUCTION

Administrators are frequently admonished to solve their organizational problems through the medium of groups. This exhortation is based largely on the body of research that demonstrates the superiority of groups over individuals in solving certain kinds of problems. Recently, however, organizational theorists have begun to point out that the

superiority of groups over individuals may be found only in undifferentiated groups, i.e., peer groups.[1] These theorists contend that in hierarchically differentiated groups, the stimulation of

---

[1] See Peter M. Blau and W. Richard Scott, *Formal Organizations* (San Francisco: Chandler, 1963); Daniel Katz and Robert L. Kahn, *The Social Psychology of Organizations* (New York: John Wiley, 1966); Louis M. Smith and Pat M. Keith, *Social Psychological Aspects of School Building Design* (Washington, D.C.: Bureau of Research, U.S. Office of Education, 1967).

* *Originally published in* Administrative Science Quarterly, *September 1968, pp. 305–319. Reprinted with permission of the publisher and the authors.*

social interaction is restricted. The validity of this contention can be tested by studying group functioning in hierarchically differentiated and undifferentiated groups.

The main purposes of the experiments reported in this paper were to determine whether hierarchically differentiated groups would be as productive on a problem-solving task as hierarchically undifferentiated groups, and to examine the effects of formally based status differences on group efficiency and risk taking.

HYPOTHESES

HYPOTHESIS 1. *Hierarchically differentiated groups will be less productive than hierarchically undifferentiated groups.* Some theorists maintain that groups are superior to individuals on certain types of problem-solving tasks, because social interaction *(1)* provides an error-correcting mechanism, *(2)* furnishes social support to individual members, and *(3)* fosters competition for respect.[2] The relationship of these factors to increased group productivity is indicated in the discussion that follows and is drawn principally from the work of Blau and Scott.[3]

It is not easy for an individual to detect mistakes in his thinking. He brings a set perspective to the problem-solving situation, which militates against his seeing the problem from another perspective. When a number of individuals are working on a common task, the chances that an error in thinking will be detected are increased, because the other people bring different assumptions, frames of references, experiences, and knowledge to bear on the problem. This facilitates the detection of false reasoning and tends to result in a rejection of ideas and suggestions based on illogical inferences.

Second, social interaction furnishes social support to group members. A problem-solving situation creates a condition of uncertainty for individual members, and this leads to mental blocks that interfere with the development of their ideas. When an individual works with a group on a task, his good suggestions are likely to receive the approval of others. Such social approval reduces his anxieties and encourages him to develop his ideas further.

Third, the presence of others motivates members of a group to make good suggestions in order to win the respect and esteem of the other members.

The presence of status differences in a group, however, curtails these three group processes, according to Blau and Scott. Formally instituted status differences undermine the competition for respect that mobilizes the energies of group members. In the face of organizationally induced status differences, there is little incentive to compete for respect, since a person's standing in the group is not based on the respect of others, but is prescribed by the formal organization. Formally instituted status differences also distort the error-correction mechanism. Subordinates are likely to be reluctant to criticize the opinions of persons with superior status or to find fault with their suggestions and ideas. Finally, formally instituted status differences affect the distribution of social support. Low-status members do not receive their share of the group's support, and it is support that relieves anxiety and stimulates thinking.

Using this line of reasoning, it is hypothesized that hierarchically differentiated groups will be less productive than undifferentiated or peer groups. The differences in the productivity of these two types of groups are accounted for by the curtailment of the three group processes in hierarchically differentiated groups.

HYPOTHESIS 2. *Hierarchically differentiated groups will be less efficient than*

---

[2] Blau and Scott, *op. cit.,* pp. 121–124.
[3] *Ibid.*

hierarchically undifferentiated groups.
When a collection of individuals comes
together in a group, the individuals
have the potential to produce more in
concert than separately; however, the
potential is not realized until a pattern
of interpersonal relations is developed.[4]
Status differences among the group
members is an obstacle that delays the
development of a pattern of interpersonal relationships. Low-status members of hierarchically differentiated
groups hesitate to become actively involved in solving the problem, until the
superordinate indicates through his behavior the kind of role he will play in
the problem-solving situation. The low-
status members define their roles in the
group and develop their pattern of behavior only after the superordinate has
made clear how he will behave in this
situation. In hierarchically undifferentiated groups, members can begin immediately to develop a pattern of interpersonal relationships, since they are
not hindered by the need to adjust and
readjust their behavior to a person with
higher formal status. This means that
the process of developing interpersonal
relationships will require more time
in hierarchically differentiated groups
than in undifferentiated groups. As a
result, the hierarchically differentiated
groups will be slower than undifferentiated groups and, therefore, less efficient in successfully moving toward the
goal.

HYPOTHESIS 3. *Hierarchically differentiated groups will exhibit less risk-taking behavior than hierarchically undifferentiated groups.* In this study,
risk-taking was measured as the willingness of group members to subject ideas
to a test. The presence of a superordinate among a group of subordinates
tends to inhibit the tendencies of subordinates to expose their ideas to possi-

---

[4] Barry E. Collins and Harold Guetz-
kow, *A Social Psychology of Group Processes for Decision-Making* (New York:
John Wiley, 1964), p. 60.

ble failure. In order for an idea to be
acted upon by the group, the person
who generates the idea must defend his
view and advocate the idea before the
rest of the group. By attempting to promote the idea, the person becomes identified with it. If the group acts upon the
idea and the idea is subsequently prov-
en unsound, the individual who advanced the idea experiences failure in
the eyes of his superior, a risk few subordinates are willing to take. It might
be expected, therefore, that hierarchically differentiated groups will present
fewer of their generated solutions to the
research worker than the undifferentiated groups. The research worker is
an immediate source of feedback concerning the worth of the idea.

METHOD

Sample

In order to test the three hypotheses, 20 groups were formed, each with
four subjects drawn from the staffs of
10 elementary schools in the St. Louis
metropolitan area. Of the 80 subjects 10
were principals (5 male and 5 female)
and 70 were teachers (68 female and 2
male). With the exception of the principals, subjects were randomly selected
from staff rosters provided to the investigators. In each of the 10 schools, two
groups were formed, each with four
members. One group included the principal and three of his teachers, while
the other group consisted of four teachers. All teachers were randomly assigned
to their groups.

The groups with the principal
were designated hierarchically differentiated groups. Status differences between the principal and his teachers
were prescribed by the formal organization. The groups composed exclusively
of teachers were designated as hierarchically undifferentiated groups. According to the organizational chart in these
schools, teachers held positions that

were equivalent in organizational status; therefore, formally based status differences were present only in the hierarchically differentiated groups.

Procedures

The small-group experiments were conducted in each of the 10 participating schools prior to and immediately following the regular school day. Hierarchically differentiated and undifferentiated groups were randomly assigned to morning and afternoon problem-solving sessions. Each session was conducted in a section of the building free of interruption. This location varied from building to building, though within each school, the location was the same for both groups.

Each subject was provided with a copy of the problem. Subjects were told to work together on it and to discuss their ideas on the solution to the problem among themselves. Participants were free to ask the experimenter questions. The only restriction imposed on their method of operation was that they had to use a parliamentarian constitutional arrangement[5] in deciding whether a solution generated by the group should be presented to the experimenter as a possible correct solution. As long as a majority of the members present agreed to present a generated solution, groups could present as many solutions as they wished, until the problem was correctly solved. Each session was tape recorded. In addition, the experimenter noted when the group overcame each one of the three beliefs, and when the group generated and presented a solution.[6] The procedure was the same for all groups.

The problem to be solved was "the doodlebug problem," a problem devised by M. Ray Denny and subsequently revised by Denny and Rokeach.[7] The problem is nonideological and is essentially a problem in logic involving an imaginary insect named Joe Doodlebug who operates in an environment under unusual governing conditions. Solution of the problem includes analysis and synthesis phases. During the analysis phase, subjects have to overcome certain presently held beliefs. In the synthesis phase subjects have to integrate the beliefs into a new system. Productivity was measured in each phase.

A time limit of 30 minutes was set for the group to solve the problem. At the close of the experimental session,

---

[5] The concept of constitutional arrangement refers to the procedures by which the group is to arrive at a decision. The three most frequently mentioned constitutional arrangements are the parliamentarian, the participant-determining, and the centralist. In groups using either the participant-determining or parliamentarian modes for reaching decisions, every group member has relatively equal power and influence over the decision. The major distinction between these modes is that under the participant-determining arrangement consensus is required. Groups using parliamentarian procedures for making and executing decisions can exercise a choice that is binding on the group whenever a majority agrees that a particular course of action is desirable. Groups operating under a centralist constitutional arrangement, are bound by a decision whenever one is reached by the person in final authority. Cf. Guy E. Swanson, The

Effectiveness of Decision-making Groups, *Adult Leadership*, 8 (June 1959), 48–52.

[6] Since each session was tape-recorded, the investigators were able to verify the accuracy of the information recorded by the experimenter during the session as to (1) the time required to overcome the first belief (the efficiency measure), (2) the number of beliefs overcome and whether the group solved the problem (the productivity measures), and (3) the number of solutions generated by the group versus the number presented as a correct solution (the risk-taking measure).

[7] For a full description of "The Doodlebug Problem," see Milton Rokeach, *The Open and Closed Mind* (New York: Basic Books, 1960), pp. 171–181.

subjects were given a copy of the solution and asked not to discuss what had occurred with anyone until the day after the last scheduled experimental session.

RESULTS

To test hypothesis 1, the differences in productivity between hierarchically differentiated and undifferentiated groups were examined in both the analysis and synthesis phases of the problem. Only three of the twenty groups solved the problem. Two of the correct solutions were generated by hierarchically undifferentiated groups; the other by a hierarchically differentiated group. The number of correct solutions was therefore too small to test differences in productivity in the synthesis phase of the task.

The hypothesis was then tested by looking at the productivity of the two kinds of groups during the analysis phase. The measure of productivity for this phase was the total number of beliefs overcome by the group in the time allotted. For each belief overcome, the group was awarded a score of one. Since there were only three beliefs—a facing belief, a direction belief, and a movement belief—to be overcome, the range on the productivity index in the analysis phase was 0 to 3.[8] The mean produc-

tivity score was 2.2 for the hierarchically differentiated groups and 2.8 for the undifferentiated groups. A test of the significance of the difference between these means resulted in a t of 2.52. For a one-tailed test with 18 df, this value is significant at the .05 level. The hypothesis is confirmed at the analysis phase of the task, the only phase that could be tested; that is, the hierarchically differentiated groups were less productive than the hierarchically undifferentiated groups.

CRITICS' NOTE:

In both "Results" and "Discussion," the investigators discussed the use of one-tailed statistical tests (as opposed to two-tailed tests). These two types of statistical test are frequently used to analyze the type of data presented in this paper. When a researcher tests the statistical significance of the difference of the mean scores for two groups, he calculates those differences (called rejection regions) which, if they occurred, would be so large as to cause him to reject the hypothesis of no difference in group means in the population—that is, to reject the hypothesis that the differences in means are due only to chance. If a researcher is willing to consider large observed differences as reason to reject this hyhothesis of no difference regardless of which group had the higher mean, the researcher is conducting a two-tailed test. (The rejection regions are at the two tails of a distribution of expected differences.) If, as the investigators of this paper have done, only large differences in favor of a specific group will lead the researcher to reject the no difference hypothesis, then a one-tailed test is being conducted.

---

[8] In the "Joe Doodlebug Problem" the subject is given the end result (that Joe must jump four times to reach his food) and is asked to tell why Joe reaches the conclusion he does. In order to reach a correct solution the subject must overcome three basic beliefs. In everyday life we face the food we are about to eat, but Joe need not face his food in order to eat it. He can land on top of it *(the facing belief)*. In everyday life we can change our direction at will. Joe, however, can change direction only by jumping sideways or backwards *(the direction belief)*. In everyday life we can change direction immediately, but Joe must make four jumps in

one direction before he changes. Subjects have difficulty with this belief because they assume that Joe is at the end rather than possibly in the middle of a sequence *(the movement belief)*.

When a one-tailed test is used, finding a difference in favor of the group NOT expected to be superior will not permit the researcher to reject the chance-alone hypothesis, no matter how large that unexpected difference is.

There is debate among statisticians over the appropriateness of one-tailed tests. The point to keep in mind is that when one-tailed tests are used, smaller group differences are needed to reject the chance-alone hypothesis provided, of course, the differences are in the direction hypothesized. This is true because one large rejection region is used rather than two smaller ones. Had the researchers used a two-tailed test, the differences in efficiency scores (hypothesis 2) and in risk-taking scores (hypothesis 3) would not have been statistically significant at the .05 level.

Hypothesis 2, comparing efficiency, was tested by examining the length of time, expressed in minutes, required to overcome the first belief. The mean number of minutes required to overcome the first belief was 2.7 for the undifferentiated groups and 4.8 for the hierarchically differentiated groups. This difference is significant at the .05 level for a one-tailed test with a t of 1.745 and df of 18. The hierarchically differentiated groups were less efficient than the undifferentiated groups.

For hypothesis 3, the operational definition of risk-taking behavior for each group was the difference between the number of solutions generated by the group and the number presented to the experimenter. The smaller the discrepancy between the number of generated solutions and presented solutions, the greater was the risk taking. The mean risk-taking score was .8 for the hierarchically undifferentiated groups and 1.8 for the hierarchically differentiated groups. The difference between the two means is significant at the .05 level for a one-tailed test, with a t of 1.754 and df of 18. Forty-four percent of the generated solutions were presented

to the experimenter in the hierarchically differentiated groups in contrast to 71 percent in the undifferentiated groups. When the administrator-generated solutions are excluded, and only the teacher generated and presented solutions are used, the difference in risk taking for the two types of groups is even more pronounced. Only 36 percent of the solutions generated by teachers in the hierarchically differentiated groups were presented to the experimenter in contrast to 71 percent in the undifferentiated groups. The presence of formally based status differences among group members did inhibit the risk-taking behabior of subordinates, as was hypothesized.

Although the investigators randomly assigned groups to morning and afternoon sessions, an analysis was made of the differences between before-school and after-school groups on each of the three dependent variables. None of the three analyses approached significance at the .05 level. The t-values for productivity, risk taking, and efficiency were all less than 1.00. The differences between the means on these three measures for morning and afternoon groups were .2 for productivity, 0 for risk taking, and .45 for efficiency.

In order to determine whether there was a significant relationship among any of the dependent variables, correlations were run on the productivity, efficiency, and risk-taking scores. None of the correlations was significant at the .05 level. The correlation coefficient for productivity and efficiency was $-.15$; for productivity and risk taking it was $-.19$. The correlation (.38) between the efficiency and the risk-taking scores does approach significance, however, and suggests that efficient groups are also high risk-taking groups.[9]

---

[9] The reader is reminded that the higher the efficiency score the more inefficient the group is and the higher the risk-taking score the fewer the risks taken by the group.

DISCUSSION

Although the results of this experiment are consistent with the hypotheses elaborated at the beginning of this paper, some questions arose during the analysis of the data. One of these questions has to do with the validity of the risk-taking index. In the hierarchically differentiated groups, although only 36 percent of the teacher-generated solutions were presented by the groups to the experimenter, 78 percent of the administrator-generated solutions were presented. One might argue that in groups with a history of association and development that the suggestions of members of lower rank are passed over more often than the suggestions of higher-ranked members.[10] If this line of reasoning is valid, then the lower proportion of solutions presented to the experimenter in the hierarchically differentiated groups was not due to a reluctance by subordinates to take risks, but rather to the tendency of ideas advanced by low-ranking group members to be overlooked. Differences between differentiated and undifferentiated groups on the risk-taking measure could be attributed to the passing over of the ideas of low-ranking members in groups having formally based status differences among the members, rather than to the hypothesized inhibition of risk taking.

In order to determine which of these two explanations might have accounted for the differences on the risk-taking index between the two types of groups, a second experiment was conducted using 18 groups, each including five subjects. Subjects for the groups were drawn from the staffs of 8 elementary schools and one junior high school in the St. Louis metropolitan area. With the exception of the principals,

---

[10] This argument was suggested in a paper by C. Heinicke and R. F. Bales, *Developmental Trends in the Structure of Small Groups*, *Sociometry*, 16 (1953), 7–38.

subjects were randomly selected from staff rosters provided the investigators. In each of the 9 schools, two groups were formed, each with five members. One group included four teachers and the principal, with the principal acting solely as an *observer*, whereas the other group consisted of five teachers, with one of the five designated as an observer. All teachers were randomly assigned to the two groups and to their roles as observer or participant. In both groups the observer was instructed to watch the group as it worked on the problem, to refrain from making any comments even if called upon by a member of the group, and to withhold any expression of emotion during the session. Though informed of the identity of the person who was designated as observer, subjects were told only that he could not participate in the problem-solving activity. No other information about the observer's role was given. The procedures during the problem-solving session were identical in other respects to the procedures followed in the first experiment.

Although information was gathered on all three measures for each group, the measure of chief interest was the scores of the two types of groups on the risk-taking measure. If this measure really represented the willingness of group members to subject ideas to a test, then the groups with a superordinate (in this case the principal) present as an observer should offer fewer of their generated solutions to the experimenter than groups with a peer serving as the observer. One the other hand, if the two types of groups did not differ on the risk-taking measure, this would argue for the interpretation that the differences on this index in the first experiment were due to the ideas of teachers (lower-status members) being overlooked when in competition with the ideas of the principal (a higher-status member).

The results of this second experiment confirmed the interpretation of the risk-taking index as a measure of the willingness of group members to subject their ideas to a test. The mean score on the risk-taking measure for groups observed by a superordinate was 1.56, while the mean score for groups observed by a peer was .56, a low score indicating high risk taking. A test of the significance of the difference between these two means resulted in a t of 2.947. For a two-tailed test with 16 df, this value is significant at the .01 level. The rival explanation for the findings in the first experiment with respect to the differences between the risk taking scores of hierarchically differentiated and undifferentiated groups was, therefore, rejected by the investigators.

A second question emerged from an analysis of the social interaction in the hierarchically differentiated groups. Since the authors had reasoned that productivity would be lower in the hierarchically differentiated groups because the stimulation of social interaction would be curtailed, the investigators studied certain aspects of the group processes to determine if these had been curtailed in the differentiated groups. Although ten such groups were tape recorded, it was possible to study the interaction processes in only eight differentiated groups because of excessive background noise. The focus of the analysis was on the extent to which the error-correction mechanism and the distribution of social support were distorted.

Distortions in the error-correction mechanism and the distribution of social support were studied by looking at what happened to ideas emanating from the principal and from one teacher randomly selected from each group. A statement by a participant was classified as an idea if it was any one of the following: *(1)* an interpretation of the problem not already mentioned in the written problem presented to the group, *(2)* a possible cause of the problem, *(3)* a possible solution of the problem, *(4)* a relationship between a cause

and a problem, and *(5)* a criterion for judging the appropriateness of any of the preceding.[11] Two investigators, working from typed transcripts of the eight sessions, independently traced what happened to each idea by looking at the three responses made immediately following the introduction of the idea.[12] The fate of each idea was classified in one of the following categories: criticized, ignored, used, accepted without being used.[13] Criticisms were considered to be the functional equivalent

---

[11] These criteria were drawn from John C. Glidewell, "Group Emotionality and Productivity" (Unpublished Ph.D. Dissertation, University of Chicago, 1953), pp. 175–76.

[12] Degree of agreement between the two coders was determind by a procedure recommended by R. F. Bales, *Interaction Process Analysis* (Cambridge, Mass.: Addison-Wesley, 1961), pp. 103–11. The extent of the agreement between coders was determined for both administrator and teacher ideas by means of the chi-square test. Bales considers a chi-square value which has a probability of .50 or greater as evidence of acceptable agreement among coders. The investigators preferred to use a more conservative estimate of agreement, and set a chi-square value with a P of .80 or greater as the acceptable level. For both the administrator and teacher ideas, the probability of a chi-square value with four degrees of freedom (unclassified responses also were included in this analysis) was in excess of .90.

[13] A response was classified as *criticized* if another participant disagreed with the idea. Disagreement could include personal judgment and/or reference to instructions and conditions. For example, a participant advances the idea that Joe will take three jumps north and then one west. Another participant then points out that Joe cannot jump diagonally. Ideas were classified as *ignored* if there was no further reference to it. An idea was classified as *used* if another participant employed the idea in developing the same or another idea or in generating a solution. For example, a participant presents the idea that Joe jumps sideways. Another participant uses

Table 1
Disposition of Ideas of Teachers and Administrators in the Hierarchically Differentiated Groups*

				Disposition of ideas				
						Acceptance		
Initiation of idea	Criticize		Use		without use		Ignore	
	%	N	%	N	%	N	%	N
Administrators	51	27	20	11	10	5	19	10
Teachers	37	20	13	7	25	14	24	13

* Chi-square test shows no significant differences at .05 level.

Table 2
Disposition of Ideas of Teachers and Administrators in the Hierarchically Differentiated and Undifferentiated Groups*

				Disposition of ideas				
						Acceptance		
Initiation of idea	Criticize		Use		without use		Ignore	
	%	N	%	N	%	N	%	N
Administrators in differentiated groups	51	27	20	11	10	5	19	10
Teachers in differentiated groups	37	20	13	7	26	14	24	13
Teachers in undifferentiated groups	35	33	23	22	22	20	20	19

* Chi-square test shows no significant differences at .05 level.

of error-correcting behavior, on the assumption that criticisms represented the rejection of false leads and unproductive ideas. Supportive behavior was signified by the use of an idea or the acceptance of an idea without use, on the assumption that these behaviors rein-

this idea by developing a solution that Joe jumps fours times, sideways to the west. An idea was coded in the *acceptance without use* category if another participant agreed with the idea, but did not use it. For example, a participant states that the size of the food is probably important. Another participant remarks, "That's right," but does not make any further comments. Slightly less than 20 percent of the ideas were clarified by the experimenter before they were used or criticized; in these cases the ideas were not classified.

forced the behavior of the person who initiated the idea, thus making him feel more secure and less anxious. An individual who set forth an idea but had it overlooked or ignored could have had his anxiety increased, if he interpreted the lack of response as representing a lack of confidence in his reasoning ability.

The disposition of administrator and teacher ideas in the hierarchically differentiated groups is reported in Table 1. A chi-square test of these data is not significant at the .05 level.

Since the disposition of an idea in the hierarchically undifferentiated groups might have differed from the disposition of an idea in the hierarchically differentiated groups, an analysis was made of what happened to the ideas emanating from a teacher randomly selected from each of eight undifferentiated groups. The results of this analysis then were contrasted with the disposition of ideas proposed by teachers and administrators in the differentiated groups in the same eight schools (see Table 2). This chi-square test also showed no significant differences in the disposition of ideas.

Differences in the level of productivity between the hierarchically differentiated and undifferentiated groups apparently were not caused by a reluctance of subordinates to criticize the ideas of superordinates as maintained by Blau and Scott in their discussion of how the error-correction mechanism operates in differentiated groups. Nor was social support, as operationally defined in this study, unevenly distributed between subordinates and superordinates in the differentiated groups as contended by Blau and Scott. Since these two conditioning variables did not operate as hypothesized, the question remains as to what accounted for the differences in the productivity of the two types of groups.

One possible explanation is that the competition for respect, a third beneficial characteristic of group processes, was curtailed by the presence of formally based status differences as Blau and Scott contend. To summarize their line of reasoning, hierarchical differentiation undermines the competition for respect. Status in the group is accorded on the basis of the person's organizational rank rather than on the basis of the person's contribution to goal attainment. One consequence of this is that members of the differentiated groups do not mobilize their energies fully and this low level of mobilization reduces group productivity.

The data in this study which suggest that members of the undifferentiated groups had more fully mobilized their energies were the number of ideas initiated by members of the two types of groups while working on the problem. This indicator, unlike the ones

used to examine distortions in the error-correction mechanism and the distribution of social support, emerged from an analysis of the data. Therefore, the data on idea initiation rates are used *post hoc* to support the competition for respect argument advanced by Blau and Scott.

Data in Table 2 indicated that a greater number of ideas were being initiated in the undifferentiated groups. To examine this possibility more systematically, an idea rate was computed for each of the groups. This idea rate was based on the total number of ideas initiated by a group divided by the amount of time the group worked on solving the problem. Significantly higher idea initiation rates were found in the hierarchically undifferentiated groups ($\overline{X} = 1.35$) than in the differentiated groups ($\overline{X} = 1.08$). This difference was significant at the .05 level for a two-tailed test ($t = 2.250$; $df = 14$).

The significantly higher idea initiation rates in the hierarchically undifferentiated groups may have been a function of the greater mobilization of energy engendered by the competition for respect in these groups. Hierarchically differentiated groups, on the other hand, may have had lower idea initiation rates because a person's standing in the group was not based upon respect gained from performance on the task. Rather, a person's standing in the group was prescribed by the formal organization. Under these conditions, competition for respect, a major determinant of a person's motivation to initiate ideas and to participate fully in accomplishing the task, was not operating.

CONCLUDING REMARKS

The findings reported in this paper tend to confirm the notion of a number of organizational theorists that hierarchical differentiation has its dysfunctioanl as well as its functional consequences. Specifically, formally based status differences were found to inhibit group productivity at the analysis phase of problem solving, efficiency, and risk taking. Hierarchical differentiation also seemed to attenuate one of the beneficial characteristics of group processes—competition for respect—as evidenced by the lower idea initiation rates.

At the same time, some doubt was cast upon two of the assumptions with which this study began, that is, that the presence of formally based status differences among group members distorts the error-correction mechanism and the distribution of social support. A more direct empirical test of these Blau and Scott postulates appears warranted, since the fate of ideas initiated by administrators and teachers in the hierarchically differentiated groups did not differ as hypothesized. It is also still a question whether differences in the productivity and efficiency of the two types of groups would be found if a centralist constitutional arrangement were used.[14] Since this type of constitutional ar-

arrangement is typically used by formal organizations in reaching decisions, a study of this variable and its effects on group performance would be meaningful. Finally, the investigators were unable to test the consequences of hierarchical differentiation at the synthesis phase of problem solving; this too represents a fruitful question for further research. Hopefully, these problems will provide productive leads for subsequent studies in the area.

---

[14] It is conceivable that the productivity of the hierarchically differentiated groups was inhibited not by formally based status differences alone but rather by a combination of formally based status differences and the constitutional arrangement chosen by the investigators. In the first experi-

ment, the investigators used a parliamentarian type of constitutional arrangement. This placed the elementary school principal in a decision-making situation with his teachers, in which the decision was to be reached by majority vote. By selecting a constitutional arrangement not customarily used in this type of organization, yet not specifying the role of the principal, the investigators may have inadvertently created a situation where the teachers did not know the appropriate status of the principal. As a result, the teachers may not have known how to behave toward the principal *in this situation*. This ambiguity may have threatened the low-power persons, leading to increased anxiety, which in turn lowered productivity. The same line of reasoning could also account for the differences between hierarchically differentiated and undifferentiated groups on the efficiency measure.

CRITIQUE

The article is divided into the following sections: "Introduction," "Hypotheses," "Method," "Results," "Discussion," and "Concluding Remarks." Evaluate the article critically, organizing your remarks into six groups to correspond to the six sections of the paper listed above. Be sure to cite strengths as well as weaknesses.

A Model Appraisal

INTRODUCTION

Although brief, the Introduction is a good one. It provides a clear idea of the content of the paper and makes a case for its significance. We believe the general problem is an important one, particularly in these times of doubt about authoritarian forms in many kinds of organization—from communes to private industry, from educational institutions and classroom groups to bureaus of the government. Further, the criteria used for judging forms of organization (i.e., productivity, efficiency, and risk taking) are important ones.

STUDENT RESPONSE. "A peer group is not necessarily undifferentiated. Peer groups hold their internal differentiation and the study does not take this into consideration."

OUR REPLY. The author does write, "undifferentiated groups, i.e., peer groups." We agree completely with the student's remarks and make this point ourselves in another context.

STUDENT RESPONSES. The Introduction is poor in that the investigators "did not present a review of the existing research," and "failed to define the hierarchically differentiated and undifferentiated groups."

OUR REPLY. Although we agree that it is important to review existing research and to define key concepts, we do not believe that it is necessary to do these things in the Introduction. The authors do refer through footnotes to the work of others in which the concept of hierarchical differentiation is described.

STUDENT RESPONSE. "The terminology was so involved that it was difficult to wade through."

OUR REPLY. Many students made similar statements, not only in regard to the Introduction but in reference to other sections as well. The investigators do have an obligation to communicate clearly; but we must remember this article is not meant for consumption by the general public. The language of science cannot be the same as everyday language for the latter is too imprecise. On the other hand, unnecessary jargon can be confusing and some balance is needed.

HYPOTHESES

The hypotheses section of this paper does not merely list the three principal hypotheses which guided the investigators' early work on the problem; it goes beyond to provide a helpful rationale for expecting the results hypothesized.

The investigators should be commended for the way in which they used social science concepts and theory to guide their research on administrative problems. This reliance on theory: (a) increases the probability that relationships will be discovered as it extends the range of relevant data looked for; (b) provides a way to explain and to account for differences when they do occur; and (c) facilitates further inquiry.

The investigators hypothesize (3) that in differentiated groups the subordinates who generate ideas will hesitate promoting them, and thus fewer of these generated ideas will be presented by the group to the research worker (there will be low risk taking). One could argue the opposite as follows: because of the greater inhibition in differentiated groups, subordinates will only suggest ideas which they feel can be defended; thus the ideas suggested in such a differentiated group are more likely to be accepted by the entire group for presentation to the research worker (there will be high risk taking).

Student Responses. "Hypothesis 3 was based on opinion." "The subjective statements used in the explanation of each hypothesis have not been proven."

Our Reply. These student readers evidently believe it not worthwhile to engage in research whose hypotheses are generated from rationales which are "opinion" and "not . . . proven." The line of reasoning behind hypotheses can range from radically speculative ideas and mere opinion to coherent rationales and logically tight theories. It may well be true that the payoff of research depends upon the location of the line of reasoning along this continuum. It is our judgment that the investigators utilized a thoughtful (if not compelling) line of reasoning which is much more than unsubstantiated opinion.

METHOD

The investigators chose to use an experimental method rather than a survey or correlational design even though in the field of educational administration the tradition of nonexperimental research is especially strong. A more usual procedure to study the effects of a variable like "hierarchical differentiation" would be to administer an instrument to identify school groups which differ naturally on this variable, and then to compare these groups with respect to the dependent variables. Our purpose in drawing this distinction is not to claim that the variable manipulating experiment conducted by the investigators is superior to the more traditional status study (although we suspect it is), but rather to highlight the fact that there is usually more than one way in which a problem can be researched.

Sample:

Ten groups, each consisting of a principal and three teachers, were classified as hierarchically differentiated. Ten other groups from the same schools, each consisting of four teachers, were classified as hierarchically undifferentiated. Thus, groups were considered hierarchically differentiated or undifferentiated solely on the basis of whether or not the principal was present.

Whether or not this distinction (hierarchically differentiated vs. undifferentiated) corresponds to the conceptual definition of "status difference" was unexamined, partly because no conceptual definition was provided. It is quite conceivable that something other than "status" was also being manipulated by the investigators, such as "maleness," "personal dominance," "differential familiarity," or "emergent vs. appointed leadership." Since status systems exist within teaching staffs, it is not certain that the all-teacher groups, supposedly without status differences, really differed on this dimension from the groups in which the principal was present. The investigators would have been well advised to check the correspondence between the operational and conceptual definitions, perhaps by means of a post-experiment questionnaire or interview.

It should be noted that the main comparison was between pairs of groups selected from the same school. Thus, differences between groups could not be attributed to school differences since the groups were essentially matched in this regard. The investigators should be commended for insuring that the basic comparison between the two types of groups was valid, even though results might not be generalizable to all types of school groups in all localities.

Procedures:

Under the section Procedures the researchers describe the problem to be solved (the doodlebug problem) and the methods of administration. The adequacy of this problem, the decision-making procedure, and the role of the experimenter deserve comment at this point.

PROBLEM ADEQUACY. One should note the difference between the doodlebug problem presented to the groups and the range of real life problems to which such groups generally attend. Many of the educational problems faced by teachers have no clear answer as does the doodlebug problem and we may therefore question whether results obtained using this special problem can be made more generally applicable. Closer inspection of the measures generated from the doodlebug problem will reveal that the problem is used to measure the ability to overcome normal beliefs rather than to measure problem-solving ability in the usual sense. The doodlebug problem is more like a puzzle than a problem in decision making.

Further, the doodlebug problem was too difficult for use in testing differences in productivity in the synthesis phase of the task. A pilot study could have shown this fact.

> Note from the investigators: *Actually, we did conduct a pilot study, and 30 minutes appeared to be ample time for solving the problem. In seeking to identify a possible cause for the unexpected outcome, we realized that we had blundered. The populations of subjects were different. Whereas the experimental subjects were teachers, the subjects in the pilot study were sophomores in the liberal arts college of a highly selective university. The implication of this situation is unmistakable; the teachers and principals in our sample were not as able as the college sophomores. We chose to safeguard the interests (namely the self-esteem) of our subjects by withholding potentially harmful information. We certainly are not the first researchers who have wrestled with the choice of what to report and what to withhold; this decision frequently arises when the objects of research are human beings.*

Finally, mention of the three beliefs to be overcome (in column 2, p. 167) well before describing them (in footnote 8 in the article) is weakness of reporting style.

Although the task was, in a sense, artificial and trivial, it does have the virtue of having been thoroughly studied in previous research and is of such a nature that principals should be as adept as teachers at solving it. This last point is important; for if the problem were something that principals could be expected to handle more easily than teachers, the group differences could be attributed to the particular skills of principals rather than to the hierarchical differentiation of the group.

Although the choice of a suitable problem was a difficult one, we believe the researchers should have chosen one or more tasks more closely related to actual school situations.

Note from the investigators: *We share the reviewers' belief that tasks more closely related to actual school situations should have been used, but feel that they have slighted a persistent dilemma faced by those choosing an experimental approach to research. An experimenter hopes to design a study which has both* internal *and* external *validity. A study is said to possess internal validity if the experimental stimulus did in fact make some significant difference in this specific instance. External validity refers to representativeness or generalizability. As Donald T. Campbell ["Factors Relevant to the Validity of Experiments in Social Settings," Psychological Bulletin, 54 (1957), 297–321], has noted:*

> *Both criteria are obviously important although it turns out that they are to some extent incompatible, in that the controls required for internal validity often tend to jeopardize representativeness. . . . If one is in a situation where either internal validity or representativeness must be sacrificed, which should it be? The answer is clear. Internal validity is the prior and indispensable consideration.*

In selecting the problem, we sought to identify one in which neither principals nor teachers would have an advantage. We were not confident that we could develop a school-related problem which could be handled with equal ease or difficulty by principals and teachers. We, therefore, sacrificed external validity in the interests of internal validity, a not uncommon sacrifice at that.

DECISION-MAKING PROCEDURES.   For purposes of reaching decisions within each group involved in the problem-solving situation, a parliamentarian arrangement in which the majority rules was decided upon. This is an unusual method for school personnel to use for reaching decisions. More likely is the centralist constitutional arrangement in which a group is bound by a decision reached by the person in final authority. As recognized by the investigators themselves (see footnote 14), use of a majority-rule procedure makes it difficult to explain the results. It is when the centralist arrangement is used that status hierarchies in groups are expected to matter most because this form recognizes and utilizes status differences in its operation. Thus, not only is the generalizability of the study weakened by use of an atypical decision-making procedure, but the very rationale for expecting status differences to be operating is less applicable to the parliamentarian arrangement and, consequently, attributing differences to status differences in the groups is very hazardous indeed.

EXPERIMENTER ROLE.   One weakness of the report is its failure to describe clearly or completely the role of the experimenter during the problem-solving sessions. It is nowhere indicated how many experimenters were used or the extent to which they had been trained for participation in the sessions. The last sentence in footnote 13 mentions that the experimenter "clarified" ideas. Elsewhere it was stated that the research worker gave immediate feedback (p. 166) and could be asked questions (p. 167). All this suggests that the experimenters may have had a more active role in the problem-solving sessions than we might have expected. It is important for us to know the exact nature of the experimenters' role more accurately to assess possible experimenter bias (or more generally, "instrumentation" effects) and the additional restraints that may have been operating on the behavior of the participants.

Finally, note that it is not made clear how the solutions of the groups were "passed on" to the experimenter. Did the administrator, when present, have any special function in the passing on activity?

STUDENT RESPONSES.   Many students mentioned the failure of the investigators to give adequate description of the following areas: (a) the doodlebug problem; (b) method for selecting the principals; (c) method for selecting the teachers, specifically if they were volunteers and why there were so many females; (d) teacher experience and age; (e) effect taping of the sessions had on inhibition; (f) fatigue of those meeting in the afternoon sessions; and (g) procedures, if any, for checking whether the morning-session teachers talked to their afternoon-session colleagues.

OUR REPLY.   (a) In our opinion, the doodlebug problem was adequately described both on page 167 and in footnote 8. Further, an accessible reference where a still more complete description can be found is provided.

(b) through (e). Printing costs are high and there are more papers than scholars have time to read. These facts argue for a judicious choice of those facts and details to be described in the research report itself. Clearly, that information which has the most bearing on the validity of the comparison between the two groups and on the generalizability of the findings should be included. For example, the investigators thought it more important to mention the name of the city than the ages of the teachers. A student argued that if the teachers differed in age they could not be considered "peers" regardless of where they were on the "organizational chart." Previous research can give us clues about what variables are likely to be important and thus worthy of description in the research report.

(f) and (g). Since treatments were randomly assigned to session times, and since small differences between sessions on the dependent variables were noted, it does not seem important to us that the fatigue and prior knowledge differences of the two groups be described.

STUDENT RESPONSES.   "Several problems of varying types should have been used." "A larger cross-section of the population should be used, and not just teaching personnel."

OUR REPLY.   These investigators wanted to make very general statements about group structure and group problem solving. It is essential that they design their research in a way that enhances the generalizability of their findings. One way they increased the generalizability of their work was by including several measures of problem-solving ability. Had they not given the same problem to all 20 groups and had they used other types of hierarchically differentiated groups (the two student suggestions quoted above) their study would have had that much more value. We do not believe that most researchers give enough thought or effort to designing studies to maximize generalizability. Ways this can be done without increasing the cost of the research are described by Millman.[1] A list of ways that research can be said to generalize is presented by Bracht and Glass.[2]

RESULTS

The Results section includes a description of the measures of the dependent variables production, efficiency, and risk taking, as well as a statistical comparison between the two types of groups on these measures.

The Measures:

PRODUCTION.   Using the number of beliefs overcome as a measure of production seems reasonable enough, although one could argue that the three beliefs should not be given equal weight.

EFFICIENCY.   Time to overcome the *first* belief is a good measure to test hypothesis 2 since it is in the early stages of group work that relative differences in speed of performance are expected. According to the investigators' predictions, developing the pattern of interpersonal relationships needed for efficient problem solving "will require more time in hierarchically differentiated groups than in undifferentiated groups [p. 166]." This time-consuming process will produce a difference in efficiency more evident in the beginning of the problem-solving situation than at the end.

The distribution of time to overcome the first belief is likely to be skewed, with a few groups taking relatively a very long time. Such groups will have a disproportionate effect on the mean of all ten or 20 groups. Further, one could argue that taking an extra minute of time early in the problem-solving effort should count more than an extra minute after the group already has worked 15 or 20 minutes. For both of these reasons, it would have been a good idea to use as the index of efficiency not time *per se* but some function of the time score such as the reciprocal of time (i.e., one divided by the time score) or logarithm of the sum, 1 plus time. Such functions have the desired properties.

---

[1] Jason Millman, "In the Service of Generalization," *Psychology in the Schools,* 1966, *3,* 333–339.

[2] Glenn Bracht and Gene Glass, "The External Validity of Experiments," *American Educational Research Journal,* 1968, *5,* 437–474.

RISK TAKING. The risk-taking measure used by the investigators is the difference between the number of generated solutions and the number presented to the experimenter. A large difference actually means low risk taking because the group seems unwilling to "risk" presenting solutions to the experimenter.

To name such a measure "risk taking" implies there is something to be lost in suggesting inaccurate solutions to the experimenter and that something is being risked in presenting other than the correct answer to the problem. Since the groups were in no way penalized for presenting such incorrect answers, what risk is involved to the *group* is not clear. The *individual* is said to risk "failure in the eyes of his superior." But this fear of failure of the individual is not reflected in the group difference score which is used as the risk-taking index. Thus, we do not believe this group risk-taking index is a measure of risk taking in the usual sense, or in the sense used in organizational theories, but more a measure of how reasonable the suggested solutions seemed to the group involved.

The definition of risk taking given by the investigators on page 169 is a stipulated definition and not an operational definition. To be an operational definition, the operations or procedures that must be followed to get the discrepancy index are needed. Of course, a researcher may give a stipulated definition of his operational definition; not all stipulated definitions are operational definitions.[3]

Statistsical Analysis:

The student should note that although 80 individuals were involved, the investigators correctly compared only the 20 group results. The group, and not the individual, is indeed the correct unit for analysis.

The likely skewness of the distribution of the "efficiency" measures has already been commented upon. The "productivity" measure also represents a skewed distribution since most of the groups must have overcome all three beliefs in order for the mean scores to be so close to the maximum score of three. Thus, as was true for the efficiency measure, a few groups which could not get off the ground, so to speak, would have a disproportionate effect on the mean productivity score for all ten groups. The investigators should have presented more of the groups' performance than merely the means.[4]

---

[3] For an extended discussion of these matters, see Part I in Robert Ennis, *Logic in Teaching* (Englewood Cliffs, N.J.: Prentice-Hall, 1969).

[4] Further, because of non-normal distributions and probable large differences in variability between the two types of groups, the mathematical assumptions of normality and homogeneity of variance underlying the proper use of the *t* test are being violated in the testing of hypotheses 1 and 2. The effect of these violations on the accuracy of the significance test may be quite minimal, however.

Note from the investigators: When the assumptions constituting the statistical model for a test are not met, doubt arises concerning the meaningfulness of a probability statement about the hypothesis in question. There is some empirical evidence to show that slight deviations from the assumptions underlying parametric tests may not have

Since the groups were matched by schools, the appropriate *t* test involves comparing 10 matched pairs instead of two independent sets of ten groups each. A different formula for computing the *t* statistic should have been used.[5]

We also take exception to the use of one-tailed tests. (Recall the Critics' Note in regard to one-tailed tests.) The use of one-tailed tests is most defensible when there is no reasonable way to explain results in favor of the hierarchically differentiated groups. For example, contrary to hypothesis 3, it might be that in hierarchically differentiated groups, generated solutions are more apt to be presented (i.e., greater risk taking exhibited) because subordinates would not want to offend their peers in front of the principal. Had two-tailed tests been used instead of one-tailed tests, the first two hypotheses in the paper would not have been statistically significant.

> Note from the investigators: *There are those who, like us, feel that a one-tailed test can be used when there is a theortical basis for a directional hypothesis (Allen L.* Edwards, Statistical Methods for the Behavioral Sciences *(New York: Holt, Rinehart & Winston, 1958); there are others, however, who feel that the potential for misusing a directional hypothesis is substantial (Gene V. Glass and Julian C. Stanley,* Statistical Methods in Education and Psychology *(Englewood Cliffs, N.J.: Prentice-Hall, 1970.) The only statement which can be made with certainty is that a debate over the merits of testing directional versus nondirectional hypotheses has raged for the past 20 years (e.g., see Cletus J. Burke, "A Brief Note on One-Tailed Tests,"* Psychological Bulletin, 50 *(1953), 384–87; and David B. Peizer, "A Note on Directional Inference,"* Psychological Bulletin, 68 *(1967), 448).*

Regardless of the *t* formula used or whether one or two-tailed tests were employed, the following interpretations seem reasonable: for each of the three dependent variables there were noticeable differences between the average performance of the groups of each type; it appears unlikely that chance alone accounts for these differences.

In paragraphs 5 and 6 on page 169, the authors performed two addi-

---

radical effects on the obtained probability figure (Sidney Siegel, *Nonparametric Statistics for the Behavioral Sciences* (New York: McGraw-Hill, 1956) and that major effects are likely to occur only when the sample is small (William L. Hays, *Statistics for Psychologists* (New York: Holt, Rinehart & Winston, 1963). What constitutes a slight deviation or a small sample is unclear, however. In light of the confused picture and to satisfy our own curiosity, we analyzed data by means of the *t* test and the Mann-Whitney *U* test, non-parametric statistic. The results were identical. As the reviewers noted, the effects may indeed be quite minimal.

[5] The different formula would have 9 degrees of freedom instead of the 18 reported by the investigators. If, on the average, the two groups from the same school were more alike in their problem-solving behavior than differentiated and undifferentiated groups from different schools (as we suspect them to be), then a higher value of *t* would result. From the data available to us, we suspect that had the investigators used the *t* formula for matched pairs the results would have been even more statistically significant.

tional analyses. They tested whether there is a difference in the dependent variables between the before-school groups and after-school groups, and they computed the correlations among the dependent variables. Had these differences or correlations been large, it would have suggested modifications in the interpretations of their results. The investigators should be commended for taking these precautions and for searching for rival explanations.

STUDENT RESPONSES.   "I really do not have enough background in statistics to evaluate this section well." "We have not covered this kind of statistics in class." "This section (due to my complete density in the area of knowledge of statistics) is impossible for me to comment on as it was all foreign to me."

OUR REPLY.   Of course the kind of discussion we gave above does require a statistical sophistication. However, do not be led into thinking that because you lack this sophistication you cannot look at the results of studies critically. Without statistical expertise you can still question whether the data presented are relevant to the questions asked. Do not give up too quickly.

STUDENT RESPONSE.   "The results didn't allow for different intelligence or personalities of individuals."

OUR REPLY.   The student could mean two things by her statement. First, she could mean that the procedures did not equate groups on intelligence or personality. To that we would reply that the random assignment of teachers to groups has the effect that such initial group differences in intelligence or personality would be due to chance alone and they can be estimated by techniques of statistical inference. Alternatively, the student could mean that the results did not provide separate analyses for individuals of different intelligence or personality. To that we would reply that such an analysis would have to be for the group as a whole (criterion scores are for the groups, not individuals within the groups). The small number of groups (ten within each treatment) would make such as analysis of limited value.

DISCUSSION

The Discussion, perhaps misnamed, consists of the investigators' attempts to provide evidence relevant to three rival hypotheses: (1) the lower proportion of solutions presented to the experimenter in the hierarchically differentiated groups was due to the tendency of ideas advanced by low-ranking members to be passed over rather than to a reluctance on the part of subordinates to take risks (pages 170–171); (2) a reluctance of subordinates to criticize the ideas of superordinates and/or an uneven distribution of social support was the reason for greater productivity in the undifferentiated groups (pp.171–173);and(3) the curtailment of competition for respect in the differentiated groups was responsible for the differences in productivity between the two types of groups.

Some of our objections to what is written in the Discussion parallel remarks made in connection with our appraisal of the Results section. Our displeasure with the risk-taking measure remains. The *t* test should have made use of the fact that the schools were matched. The chi-square tests are inappropriate since the responses of the same person are represented by more than one frequency in the table and thus the independence assumption underlying the proper use of the chi-square test was violated.

Perhaps most disconcerting is the investigators' belief that the number of ideas initiated as a measure of the degree to which group energies are mobilized is a serious test of the competition for respect explanation. We wonder why the investigators are so willing to accept Blau and Scott's third explanatory factor after they rejected the first two.

STUDENT RESPONSE. "In the second experiment, it was wrong to have the principal as an observer. He will have a certain effect on the situation."

OUR REPLY. Recall that the purpose of the additional study was to determine if ". . . the lower proportion of solutions presented to the experimenter in the hierarchically differentiated groups was not due to a reluctance by subordinates to take risks, but rather to the tendency of ideas advanced by low-ranking group members to be overlooked [p. 170]." To determine which of these is more likely it was necessary, as the investigators did, to design a situation in which the same reluctance by subordinates to take risks was possible (i.e., principal present) but one in which the principal has no chance to overlook subordinates' ideas (i.e., present but no active role).

CONCLUDING REMARKS

The phrase "tend to confirm" in the first sentence under the Concluding Remarks section is too strong. "Confirm" suggests that the evidence is now sufficient to warrant acceptance of the conclusion. We do not believe the investigators meant to give such assurance.

We commend the investigators for mentioning ways in which the research is still incomplete (e.g., they did not investigate centralist constitutional arrangement or problem solving at the synthesis phase) and for pointing to needed research on the topic.

A SUMMARY OF OUR ASSESSMENT

The problem the investigators set out to study is an important one and their study provides a good illustration of the close and sensitive integration of theory and data. We see the choice of the doodlebug problem as an unfortunate one, and we would have liked to have seen evidence that they successfully manipulated the hierarchical differentiation variable. The investigators did take pains not only to test their predictions but also to examine the assumptions upon which their predictions were based. We believe that the investigators went about their research business in order to protect themselves from improper inference and not just to convince others that they had conducted their study properly.